Boredom

A Philosophy of Boredom

Lars Svendsen

Translated by John Irons

REAKTION BOOKS

Published by Reaktion Books Ltd
Unit 32, Waterside
44–48 Wharf Road
London N1 7UX, UK

www.reaktionbooks.co.uk

First published in English 2005, reprinted 2005, 2006, 2011
Transferred to digital printing 2013

This book was first published in 1999 by Universitetsforlaget, Oslo,
under the title *Kjedsomhetens filosofi* by Lars Fr. H. Svendsen
© Universitets Forlaget

English-language translation © Reaktion Books 2005
This translation has been published with the financial support
of NORLA Non-fiction.

English translation by John Irons

Printed and bound in the USA
by University of Chicago Press

British Library Cataloguing in Publication Data

Svendsen, Lars Fr. H., 1970–
A philosophy of boredom
1. Boredom   2. Boredom in literature
I.Title
152.4

ISBN: 978 1 86189 217 1

Contents

Preface

My reason for writing this book was this: I was deeply bored for a while. What made me realise the importance of the topic, however, was the boredom-related death of a close friend. I came to the point where I had to agree with Rimbaud: 'boredom is no longer my love'.[1] Being bored was no longer merely an innocent pose or a minor infliction. Rimbaud's complaint of 'dying of boredom'[2] – later to be repeated in numerous pop and rock songs from G. G. Allin's *Bored to death* to Depeche Mode's *Something to do* – suddenly became real. These songs stood out as the soundtracks of our lives. I believed that this experience was not restricted to a close circle of friends but rather indicated a serious problem regarding *meaning* in our contemporary culture as a whole. To investigate the problem of boredom is to attempt to understand who we are and how we fit into the world at this particular point in time. The more I thought about it, the more boredom seemed to be seminal for understanding contemporary culture. We live in a culture of boredom, and *A Philosophy of Boredom* is my modest attempt to come to terms with that culture.

At a more academic level, I was motivated by a certain dissatisfaction with contemporary philosophy. Emmanuel Levinas describes contemporary thought as one that passes through a world without human traces.[3] Boredom, on the other hand, is human – all too human.

This book was originally written as an essay at a time when I had planned to devote myself to leisure. After having completed a lengthy research project, I was going to relax and do . . . *nothing*. But that turned out to be absolutely impossible to carry out. Obviously, I was unable to do nothing. So I thought I had better do something, hence this book.

Most often, we do not have any well-developed concepts for that which torments us. Very few people indeed have any well-thought-out concept of boredom. It is usually a blank label applied to everything that fails to grasp one's interest. Boredom is first and foremost something we live with, not so much something we think about systematically. Even so, we can attempt to develop certain concepts about boredom so as to understand better what it is that afflicts us when it strikes. This book is an attempt to develop such thoughts about what boredom is, when it arose, why it did so, why it afflicts us, how it does so and why it cannot be overcome by any act of will.

But let me say that although everything in this book is thematized in terms of the *relation* it has to boredom, it is clear that boredom is only one aspect of human existence. My intention is in no way to reduce all of life to being an expression of boredom.

It is important to find the right form for the subject to be dealt with. I once began to read a philosophical article on love. After a few lines the following statement came up: 'Bob loves Kate if, and only if . . .'. At that point, I stopped reading. Such a formalized approach was unsuitable for treating a subject like love, because the actual phenomenon would in all probability be lost in the process. So the reader ought not to expect such statements as: 'Peter is bored if, and only if . . .'. As Aristotle points out, we cannot seek to attain the same level of precision in all subjects; we must make do with the level that the subject-matter itself permits. Boredom is a vague, diverse phenomenon, and I believe that a long essay is the most suitable form for an investigation of it, not a strictly analytical dissertation. So I intend to present less of a cohesive argument, more a series of sketches that will hopefully bring us closer to an understanding of boredom. Since the phenomenon is so diverse, it calls for an interdisciplinary approach. So I have based myself on texts from many different disciplines, such as philosophy, literature, psychology, theology and sociology.

The book consists of four main sections: Problem, Stories, Phenomenology, Ethics. In the first I give a broad account of various aspects of boredom and its relationship to modernity. The second is devoted to a presentation of certain stories concerning boredom. A central thesis here is that Romanticism constitutes the most central basis, in terms of the history of ideas, for an understanding of modern boredom. The third focuses on Martin Heidegger's phenomenological investigations of boredom, and in the fourth I discuss what stance one can adopt to boredom as well as how one ought *not* to do so. There is a loose thread that runs throughout these four sections, although each can be read independently.

I have attempted to write this book in a non-technical style, as boredom is an experience that affects many people, plus I want this book to be accessible. Even so, certain passages are quite demanding – this is simply due to the fact that the subject at times *is* demanding. In the course of writing, comments from friends and colleagues have been invaluable. I thank them for their contribution, and, not least, for having put up with me at a time when I was virtually unable to talk about anything else other than the subject of this book. A special thanks must go to Ståle Finke, Ellen-Marie Forsberg, Anne Granberg, Helge Jordheim, Thomas Nilsen, Hilde Norrgrén, Erik Thorstensen and Knut Olav Åmås for their detailed comments on the typescript.

ONE

The Problem of Boredom

BOREDOM AS A PHILOSOPHICAL PROBLEM

As a philosopher, from time to time one must attempt to address big questions. If one fails to do so, one loses sight of what led one to study philosophy in the first place. In my opinion, boredom is one such big question, and an analysis of boredom ought to say something important about the conditions under which we live. We ought not – and are actually unable to – avoid considering our attitude towards the question of *being* from time to time. There may be many initial reasons for reflecting on one's life, but the special thing about fundamental existential experiences is that they inevitably lead one to question one's own existence. Profound boredom is one fundamental existential experience. As Jon Hellesnes has asked: 'What can possibly be more existentially disturbing than boredom?' [1]

The big questions are not necessarily the eternal questions, for boredom has only been a central cultural phenomenon for a couple of centuries. It is of course impossible to determine precisely *when* boredom arose, and naturally it has its precursors. But it stands out as being a typical phenomenon of modernity. On the whole, the precursors were restricted to small groups, such as the nobility and the clergy, whereas the boredom of modernity is wide-ranging in its effect and can be said to be a relevant phenomenon today for practically everyone in the Western world.

Boredom is usually considered as something random in relation to the nature of man, but this is based on highly dubious assumptions regarding human nature. One could just as well claim that boredom is embodied in human nature, but that would also presuppose that there is anything at all that can be called 'human nature' – a presupposition that seems problematic to me. Postulating a given nature has a tendency to put an end to all further discussion. For, as Aristotle points out, we direct our attention first and foremost to that which is capable of change.[2] By postulating a *nature* we are claiming that it cannot be changed. It can also be tempting to postulate a completely neutral human nature, where man has just as great a potential to experience sadness as happiness, enthusiasm as boredom. In that case, the explanation of boredom is exclusively to be found in the individual's social environment. I do not believe, however, that a clear distinction can be made between psychological and social aspects when dealing with a phenomenon such as boredom, and a reductive sociologism is just as untenable as a psychologism. So I choose to approach the matter from a different angle, adopting a perspective based partly on the history of ideas and partly on phenomenology. Nietzsche pointed out that the 'hereditary fault of all philosophers' is to base themselves on man at a particular period of time and then turn this into an eternal truth.[3] So I will make do with stating that boredom is a very serious phenomenon that affects many people. Aristotle insisted that virtue is not natural, but that it is not unnatural either.[4] The same applies to boredom. Moreover, an investigation of boredom can be carried out without presupposing any anthropological constants, i.e., anything given independently of a specifically social and historical space. We are dealing here with an investigation of man in a particular historical situation. It is *us* I am writing about, living in the shadow of Romanticism, as inveterate Romantics without the hyperbolic faith of Romanticism in the ability of the imagination to transform the world.

Even though all good philosophy ought to contain an important element of self-knowledge, it does not necessarily have to take the form of a confession modelled on Augustine's *Confessions*. Many people have asked me if I undertook this project because I suffered from boredom, but what I personally feel ought not to be of any interest to readers.[5] I do not conceive philosophy as being a confessional activity, rather one that labours to gain clarity – a clarity that is admittedly never more than temporary – in the hope that the small area one feels one has shed light on will also be of relevance to others. From a philosophical point of view, my private conditions are irrelevant, even though they are naturally important to me.

I carried out a small, unscientific survey among colleagues, students, friends and acquaintances that revealed that they were on the whole unable to say whether they were bored or not, although some answered in the affirmative or the negative – and one person even claimed that he had *never* been bored. To those readers who have possibly never been bored I can say by way of comparison that deep boredom is related, phenomenologically speaking, to insomnia, where the I loses its identity in the dark, caught in an apparently infinite void. One tries to fall asleep, takes perhaps a few faltering steps, but does not gain sleep, ending up in a no man's land between a waking state and sleep. In *Book of Disquiet* Fernando Pessoa wrote:

> Certain sensations are slumbers that fill up our mind like a fog and prevent us from thinking, from acting, from clearly and simply being. As if we hadn't slept, something of our undreamed dreams lingers in us, and the torpor of the new day's sun warms the stagnant surface of our senses. We're drunk on not being anything, and our will

is a bucket poured out onto the yard by the listless movement of a passing foot.[6]

Pessoa's boredom is obvious – it is distinct in all its form-
lessness. It is, however, in the nature of things that very few
people indeed can come up with an unequivocal answer as
to whether they are bored or not. First, moods, generally
speaking, are seldom intentional subjects as far as we are
concerned – they are precisely something one finds oneself
in, not something one consciously looks *at*. And second,
boredom is a mood that is typified by a lack of quality that
makes it more elusive than most other moods. Georges
Bernanos's village priest provides us with a fine description
of the imperceptibly destructive nature of boredom in *The
Diary of a Country Priest*:

> So I said to myself that people are consumed by bore-
> dom. Naturally, one has to ponder for a while to realise this
> – one does not see it immediately. It is a like some sort of
> dust. One comes and goes without seeing it, one breathes it
> in, one eats it, one drinks it, and it is so fine that it doesn't
> even scrunch between one's teeth. But if one stops up for a
> moment, it settles like a blanket over the face and hands.
> One has to constantly shake this ash-rain off one. That is
> why people are so restless.[7]

It is perfectly possible to be bored without being aware of
the fact. And it is possible to be bored without being able
to offer any reason or cause for this boredom. Those who
claimed in my small survey that they were deeply bored were
as a rule unable to state accurately *why* they were bored; it
wasn't this or that that plagued them, rather a nameless,
shapeless, object-less boredom. This is reminiscent of what
Freud said about melancholy, where he began by stressing
a similarity between melancholy and grief, since both contain

an awareness of loss. But whereas the person who grieves always has a distinct object of loss, the melancholic does not precisely know what he has lost.[8]

Introspection is a method that has obvious limitations when investigating boredom, so I decided to look critically at a number of texts of a philosophical and literary nature. I regard literature as excellent source-material for philosophical studies, and for the philosophy of culture it is just as indispensable as scientific works are for the philosophy of science. As a rule, literature is a great deal more illuminative than quantitative sociological or psychological studies. This applies not least to our subject, where much research has focused on how the deficiency or surplus of sensory stimuli cause boredom without this always being particularly illuminative when considering such a complex phenomenon as boredom.[9] As Adam Phillips, a psychoanalyst, has expressed it: 'Clearly, we should speak not of boredom, but of boredoms, because the notion itself includes a multiplicity of moods and feelings that resist analysis.'[10]

It is often claimed that about ten per cent of us suffer from depression in the course of life. What is the difference between profound boredom and depression? My guess is that there is a considerable overlap. I would also guess that almost one hundred per cent of the population suffers from boredom in the course of their life. Boredom cannot simply be understood as a personal idiosyncrasy. It is a much too comprehensive phenomenon to be explained away in such a way. Boredom is not just an inner state of mind; it is also a characteristic of the world, for we participate in social practices that are saturated with boredom. At times, it almost seems as if the entire Western world has become like Berghof, the sanatorium Hans Castorp stayed at for seven years in Thomas Mann's novel *The Magic Mountain*. We kill time and bore ourselves to death. So it can be tempting to agree with Lord Byron: 'There's little left but to be bored or bore.'[11]

My small survey revealed that there were more men than women who claimed to have been bored. Psychological investigations also indicate that men suffer more from boredom than women.[12] (These investigations also support Schopenhauer's claim that the feeling of boredom diminishes with age.[13]) I have no good explanation as to why this should be the case. It may be that women to a lesser extent than men verbally *express* boredom, but that they are affected by it to an equal extent. Possibly, women have other needs and sources of meaning than men and are therefore less affected by various cultural changes that give rise to boredom. As mentioned, I have been unable to find any satisfactory explanation of this gender difference. Nietzsche too claims that women suffer less from boredom than men, motivating this by saying that women have never learnt to work properly [14] – a more than dubious form of justification.

I think Kierkegaard exaggerated when he claimed that 'Boredom is the root of all evil.'[15] But it contributes to a great deal of evil. I do not believe that all murders start because of boredom, for they are known most often to be acts of passion, but it is a fact that boredom is often cited as the reason for a number of crimes committed – including murder. Nor can we say that wars start because of boredom, although it is a fact that the outbreak of some wars has been accompanied by manifest joy, with euphoric crowds filling the streets, as if celebrating the fact that something has finally broken the monotony of everyday life. Jon Hellesnes has written perceptively about this.[16] The problem about war, however, is that it is not only deadly but that it also quickly becomes deadly boring; 'Wars without interest boredom of a hundred years' wars',[17] wrote Pound. In *The Magic Mountain* it is the outbreak of war that finally wakens Hans Castorp from his seven-year slumber, but there is every reason to believe that Castorp is soon to be afflicted by boredom once more. In an attempt to say at least *something* positive about boredom, the sociologist Robert Nisbet has claimed that boredom is not only the root of a number of evils but that it has also put an end to a number of evils, for the simple reason that they gradually became too boring. He takes the practise of burning of witches as an example, claiming that it did not die out for legal, moral or religious reasons but simply because it had become too boring, and that people thought: 'If you've seen one burn, you've seen them all.'[18] Nisbet possibly has a point here, although boredom can scarcely be said to be a redeeming force. For implicit in his argument is the idea that boredom was also the cause of witch-burning beginning in the first place.

Boredom has become associated with drug abuse, alcohol abuse, smoking, eating disorders, promiscuity, vandalism, depression, aggression, animosity, violence, suicide, risk behaviour, etc. There are statistical grounds for making the connection.[19] This ought not to surprise anyone, for the Early Fathers of the Church were already well aware of such a connection, considering the pre-modern forerunner of boredom, *acedia*, to be the worst sin, since all other sins derived from it. That boredom has serious consequences for a society, not only for individuals, ought to be beyond all doubt. That it is also serious for individuals is because boredom involves a loss of meaning, and a loss of meaning is serious for the afflicted person. I do not believe that we can say that the world appears to be meaningless because one is bored, or that one is bored because the world appears to be meaningless. There is hardly a simple relationship here between a cause and an effect. But boredom and a loss of meaning are connected in some way. In *The Anatomy of Melancholy* (1621), Robert Burton claimed that 'we can talk about 88 degrees of melancholy, since diverse people are diversely attacked and descend deeper or are dipped less deeply in the hellish pit.' Personally, I am unable to distinguish all that precisely between various degrees of boredom, but it covers everything from a slight discomfort to a serious loss of all meaning. For most of us, boredom is bearable – but not for all. It is of course always tempting to ask the person complaining of boredom or melancholy to 'pull himself together', but, as Ludvig Holberg points out, this is 'just as impossible to do as ordering a dwarf to make himself one cubit taller than he is'.[20]

Almost all those who talk about boredom consider boredom to be an evil, although there are certain exceptions. Johann Georg Hamann described himself as a 'Liebhaber der Langen Weile', and when his friends criticized him for being a good-for-nothing, he replied that it is easy to work, whereas genuine idleness is really demanding on a human being.[21] E. M. Cioran has a similar view: 'To the friend who tells me he is bored because he is unable to work, I reply that boredom is a *superior* state, and that it is debasing it to connect it with the notion of work.'[22]

There are no courses offered at the universities, apart from the fact that one is often bored during one's studies. Nor is it obvious that boredom can any more be considered a relevant philosophical subject, although it has formerly been so. In a contemporary philosophy where almost everything has become variations on the theme of epistemology, boredom would seem to be a phenomenon that falls outside the framework of philosophy as a discipline. To busy oneself with such a subject will for some people be seen as a clear indication of intellectual immaturity. That may well be. If boredom cannot be considered a relevant philosophical subject nowadays, there is perhaps good reason to be concerned about the state of philosophy. A philosophy that cuts itself off from the question of the meaning of life is hardly worth getting involved in. That meaning is something we can lose falls outside the framework of philosophical semantics, but it ought not to fall outside the framework of philosophy as a whole.

Why should boredom be a *philosophical* problem and not just a psychological or sociological problem? I have to admit here that I am unable to advance any general criterion as to what distinguishes a philosophical problem from a non-philosophical one. According to Wittgenstein, a philosophical problem has the form: 'I don't know my way about.' [23] Similarly, Martin Heidegger describes the 'need' that drives one to philosophical reflection as a 'not-inside-out-knowledge'.[24] What characterizes a philosophical question, then, is some sort of loss of bearings. Is this not also typical of profound boredom, where one is no longer able to find one's bearings in relation to the world because one's very relationship to the world has virtually been lost? Samuel Beckett describes this existentialist state embodied in his character hero, Belacqua, in this way:

> He was bogged in indolence, without identity . . . The cities and forests and beings were also without identity, they were shadows, they exerted neither pull nor goad . . . His being was without axis or contour, its centre everywhere and periphery nowhere, an unsurveyed marsh of sloth.[25]

Boredom normally arises when we cannot do what we want to do, or have to do something we do not want to do. But what about when we have no idea of what we want to do, when we have lost the capacity to get our bearings in life? Then we can find ourselves in a profound boredom that is reminiscent of a lack of willpower, because the will cannot get a firm grip anywhere. Fernando Pessoa has described this as 'To suffer without suffering, to want without desire, to think without reason.' [26] And, as we shall see in the analysis of Heidegger's phenomenology of boredom, this experience can be a way into philosophy.

Boredom lacks the charm of melancholy – a charm that is connected to melancholy's traditional link to wisdom, sensitivity and beauty. For that reason, boredom is less attractive to aesthetes. It also lacks the obvious seriousness of depression, so it is less interesting to psychologists and psychiatrists. Compared to depression and melancholy, boredom simply seems to be too trivial or vulgar to merit a thorough investigation. It is surprising, for example, that Peter Wessel Zapffe's 600-page study *On the Tragic* (1941) contains not a single discussion of boredom.[27] Zapffe admittedly touches on the phenomenon at various points, but it is not given its usual name. We do, however, find discussions of boredom by important philosophers, such as Pascal, Rousseau, Kant, Schopenhauer, Kierkegaard, Nietzsche, Heidegger, Benjamin and Adorno. And within literature there are Goethe, Flaubert, Stendhal, Mann, Beckett, Büchner, Dostoevsky, Chekhov, Baudelaire, Leopardi, Proust, Byron, Eliot, Ibsen, Valéry, Bernanos, Pessoa . . . This list is incomplete – the subject is so comprehensively described that any such list is arbitrary. We ought, however, to note that all these writers and philosophers belong to the modern period.

BOREDOM AND MODERNITY

According to Kierkegaard, 'The gods were bored; therefore they created human beings. Adam was bored because he was alone; therefore Eve was created. Since that moment, boredom entered the world and grew in quantity in exact proportion to the growth of population.'[28] Nietzsche's view was that God was bored on the seventh day,[29] and he claimed that even the gods fought in vain against boredom.[30] Henry David Thoreau supported Kierkegaard's idea ('Without a doubt, the form of boredom and lassitude that imagines it has exhausted all the happiness and variety of life is just as old as Adam.'[31]), and Alberto Moravia claimed that Adam and Eve were bored,[32] whereas Kant asserted that Adam and Eve *would have* been bored if they had stayed in Paradise.[33]

Robert Nisbet decided that God banished Adam and Eve from Paradise to save them from the boredom that in time would have afflicted them.[34]

It is reasonable to assume that certain forms of boredom have existed since the beginning of time, among them that which will be discussed later as 'situative boredom', i.e., a boredom that is due to something specific in a situation. But *existential* boredom stands out as being a phenomenon of modernity. There are exceptions here too. Take, for example, the opening chapter of Ecclesiastes that contains the statement 'All is vanity . . .' and also 'The thing that hath been, it is that which shall be; and that which is done is that which shall be done: and there is no new thing under the sun.' [35] It is not unreasonable, however, to say that Solomon is here being prophetic rather than diagnostic on behalf of his age. And Pastor Løchen in Arne Garborg's *Weary Men* seems to be right in claiming that this Old Testament book was written for the people of the present age.[36] There are also writings by Seneca where via the concept *tedium vitae* (tiredness of life) he describes something that is strongly reminiscent of modern boredom.[37] It is practically always possible to find earlier texts that seem to anticipate later phenomena. I do not assert that there is any clear, sharp break at any point in history, but insist that boredom is not thematized to any *major* extent before the Romantic era. With the advent of Romanticism, boredom becomes, so to speak, democratized and finds a broad form of expression.

Boredom is the 'privilege' of modern man. While there are reasons for believing that joy and anger have remained fairly constant throughout history, the amount of boredom seems to have increased dramatically. The world has apparently become more boring. Before Romanticism it seems to have been a marginal phenomenon, reserved for monks and the nobility. For a long time boredom was a status symbol, i.e., as long as it was a prerogative of the upper echelons of society, since they were the only ones with the material basis required for boredom. As boredom spread to all social strata it lost its exclusiveness. There are further reasons for believing that boredom is fairly equally distributed throughout the Western world.

Boredom always contains a critical element,[38] because it expresses the idea that either a given situation or existence as a whole is deeply unsatisfying. As François de La Rochefoucauld already pointed out in his Maxims – which are mainly acute descriptions of life at the French court – 'Almost always we are bored by people to whom we ourselves are boring'.[39] At the French court, boredom was the privilege of the monarch, for if another member of the court expressed boredom, it could scarcely be interpreted in any other way than that the monarch bored that particular person. Similarly, the earlier *acedia* had to be considered as an unprecedented insult to God when the monks sank into a fathomless void in their meeting with Holy Writ. How could God, in His perfection, ever be thought of as boring? To be bored in relation to God is implicitly claiming that God *lacks* something.

If boredom increases, it means that there is a serious fault in society or culture as a conveyor of meaning. Meaning has to be understood as a whole. We become socialized within an overall meaning (no matter what form this takes) that gives meaning to the individual elements in our lives. Another traditional expression of such an overall meaning is 'culture'. Many theoreticians of modernity have concluded that culture has disappeared and that it has been replaced, for example, by 'civilization'.[40] If boredom increases, this is presumably because the overall meaning has disappeared. There naturally is a mutual relationship between the overall meaning and the submeanings, i.e., between culture on the one hand and cultural products on the other – and we can also ask ourselves to what extent things are still bearers of culture. Do things still thing?, to quote Heidegger. To put it another way: Do the things have a cohesive influence on a culture?

There are no completely reliable studies of how large a percentage of the population is bored, the figures varying considerably for the different studies, for the phenomenon is difficult to diagnose in any objective way.[41] So we cannot, on the evidence of 'hard facts', decide whether boredom is decreasing, increasing or stable in the population. But are not the extent of the entertainments industry and the consumption of intoxicants, for example, clear indications of the prevalence of boredom? People who watch TV four hours a day will not necessarily feel or admit that they are bored, but why else should they spend 25 per cent of their waking hours in such a way? Leisure naturally presents itself as an explanation, but leisure gives one a great deal of superfluous time that has to be consumed in some way or other – and few types of apparatus destroy time more efficiently than a TV. There is ultimately hardly any other reason for watching TV for many hours an evening than to get rid of time that is superfluous or disagreeable. At the same time, many of us have gradually become terribly proficient at getting rid of time. The most hyperactive of us are precisely those who have the lowest boredom thresholds. We have an almost complete lack of downtime, scurrying from one activity to the next because we cannot face tackling time that is 'empty'. Paradoxically enough, this bulging time is often frighteningly empty when viewed in retrospect. Boredom is linked to a way of *passing the time*, in which time, rather than being a horizon for opportunities, is something that has to be beguiled. Or, as Hans-George Gadamer expresses it: 'What is actually passed when passing the time? Not time, surely, that passes? And yet it is time that is meant, in its empty lastingness, but which as *something* that lasts is too long and assumes the form of painful boredom.'[42] One does

23

not know what to do with time when one is bored, for it is precisely there that one's capacities lie fallow and no real opportunities present themselves.

It is revealing to look at the frequency of the use of the word *boredom*. It is not found in English before the 1760s, since when its usage has progressively increased.[43] The German *Langeweile* was on the scene a couple of decades earlier, and admittedly has Old-German precursors, but these only denote a long period of time, not any experiencing of time. The Danes were quick off the mark with *kedsomhed*, which is first registered in an undated, handwritten dictionary by Matthias Moth (*c*. 1647–1719);[44] it is conceivable that the Danish *ked* is etymologically related to the Latin *acedia*. Generally speaking, the words that denote boredom etc. in various languages have uncertain etymologies. The French *ennui* and the Italian *noia*, both of which, via the Provençal *enojo*, have roots in the Latin *inodiare* (to hate or detest), go back as far as the thirteenth century. But these words are less usable for our purpose, because they are closely meshed with *acedia*, melancholy and general *tristesse*. The same applies to the English word *spleen*, which goes back to the sixteenth century. The standard dictionary of the Norwegian language does not mention any earlier occurrence of *kjedsomhet* than in the works of Ibsen and Amalie Skram, although it would be very surprising if there are no earlier uses of it.[45] The earliest Norwegian 'boredom novel' is probably Arne Garborg's *Weary Men* (1891), which deals with Gabriel Gram's life, one lived constantly on the run from boredom, and Gram's yearning for release, either in the form of woman or God. On the whole, I have chosen to restrict myself to *boredom*, *Langeweile* and *kjedsomhet*, because they appear at approximately the same time and are more or less synonymous. It is obvious, however, that they belong to a large conceptual complex with long historical roots.

The word *boring* is used incredibly frequently to denote a range of emotional limitations and lack of meaning in various situations. Many descriptions of boredom in literature are extremely similar, mainly consisting of a statement that there is nothing that can engender any interest, along with a complaint at how unliveable this makes life. Kierkegaard described it thus:

> How frightful boredom is – frightfully boring; I know of no stronger expression, no truer expression, for only like knows like. If only there were a higher expression, a stronger one; that would at least indicate a shift. I lie outstretched, inactive; the only thing I see is: emptiness; the only thing I live off: emptiness; the only thing I move in: emptiness. I do not even experience pain.[46]

Here, too, I can mention Iggy Pop's song *I'm bored*, which includes the following:

> I'm bored
> I'm bored
> I'm the chairman of the bored
> I'm sick
> I'm sick of all my kicks
> I'm sick of all the stiffs
> I'm sick of all the dips
> I'm bored
> I bore myself to sleep at night
> I bore myself in broad daylight
> 'Cause I'm bored
> I'm bored
> Just another dirty bore . . .

Boredom is apparently a concept that can be used to explain or even excuse a great deal. Dostoevsky's underground man, for example, claims that 'everything stemmed from boredom'.[47] It is common to use boredom as an excuse for most things. A typical formulation is to be found in Georg Büchner's novella *Leonce und Lena*: 'What do people not invent out of boredom! [48] They study out of boredom, play out of boredom, and finally they die out of boredom.' An even stronger version is found in Büchner's more tragic *Lenz*: 'Most people play out of sheer boredom, some fall in love out of boredom, others are virtuous, yet others dissolute. As for me, nothing at all – I don't even feel like taking my own life, it's all too boring.' [49] Similarly, Stendhal writes in *On Love*: 'Ennui takes everything from one, even the desire to take one's own life.' [50] For Fernando Pessoa, boredom is said to be so radical that it cannot even be overcome by suicide, only by something completely impossible - not to have existed at all.[51] Boredom is used as an explanation for all sorts of action and for a total incapacity for action. Boredom underlies the vast majority of human actions of both a positive and negative nature. For Bertrand Russell, 'Boredom as a factor in human behaviour has received, in my opinion, far less attention than it deserves. It has been I believe, one of the great motive powers throughout the historical epoch, and it is so at the present day more than ever.' [52]

BOREDOM AND MEANING

That boredom is probably more widespread than ever before can be established by noting that the number of 'social placebos' is greater than it has ever been.[53] If there are more substitutes for meaning, there must be more meaning that needs to be substituted for.[54] Where there is a lack of personal meaning, all sorts of diversions have to create a substitute – an ersatz-meaning. Or the cult of celebrities, where one gets completely engrossed in the lives of others because one's own life lacks meaning. Is our fascination with the bizarre, fed daily by the mass media, not a result of our awareness of the boring? The pell-mell rush for diversions precisely indicates our fear of the emptiness that surrounds us. This rush, the demand for satisfaction and the lack of satisfaction are inextricably intertwined. The more strongly individual life becomes the centre of focus, the stronger the insistence on meaning amongst the trivialities of everyday life will become. Because man, a couple of centuries ago, began to see himself as an individual being that must *realize* himself, everyday life now appears to be a prison. Boredom is not connected with actual needs but with desire. And this desire is a desire for sensory *stimuli*. Stimuli are the only 'interesting' thing.

That life to a large extent *is* boring is revealed by our placing such great emphasis on originality and innovation.[55] We place greater emphasis nowadays on whether something is 'interesting' than on whether it has any 'value'. To consider something exclusively from the point of view of whether it is 'interesting' or not is to consider it from a purely aesthetic perspective. The aesthetic gaze registers only surface, and this surface is judged by whether it is interesting or boring. To what extent something lands up in the one category or the other will often be a question of potency of effect: if a piece of recorded music seems boring, it sometimes helps to turn up the volume. The aesthetic gaze has to be titillated by increased intensity or preferably by something new, and the ideology of the aesthetic gaze is superlativism. It is, however, worth noting that the aesthetic gaze has a tendency to fall back into boredom – a boredom that defines the entire content of life in a negative way, because it is that which has to be avoided at any price. This was perhaps particularly evident in postmodern theory, where we saw a series of *jouissance* aesthetes, with such mantras as 'intensity', 'delirium' and 'euphoria'. The problem was that the postmodern state was not all that euphoric and joyful for very long. It soon became boring.

We cannot adopt a stance towards something without there being an underlying interest, for interest provides the direction.[56] But, as Heidegger emphasised, today's interest is only directed towards the *interesting*, and the interesting is what only a moment later one finds indifferent or boring.[57] The word 'boring' is bound up with the word 'interesting'; the words become widespread at roughly the same time and they increase in frequency at roughly the same rate.[58] It is not until the advent of Romanticism towards the end of the eighteenth century that the demand arises for life to be interesting, with the general claim that the self must realize itself. Karl Philipp Moritz, whose importance for German Romanticism has only recently been truly recognized, claimed in 1787 that a connection between interest and boredom exists, and that life must be interesting to avoid 'unbearable boredom'.[59] The 'interesting' always has a brief shelf-life, and really no other function than to be consumed, in order that boredom can be kept at arm's length. The prime commodity of the media is 'interesting information' – signs that are pure consumer goods, nothing else.

In his essay 'The Narrator', Walter Benjamin insisted that 'experience has fallen in value'.[60] This is connected to the emergence of a new form of communication in high-capitalism: *information*. 'Information [. . .] lays claim to prompt verifiability. The prime requirement is that it appear "understandable in itself" [. . .] no event any longer comes to us without already being shot through with explanation.'[61] While experience gives personal meaning, this is undermined by information.[62] At about the same time as Benjamin made his observation, T. S. Eliot wrote:

Where is the Life we have lost in living?
Where is the wisdom we have lost in knowledge?

Where is the knowledge we have lost in information? [63]

We know that information and meaning are not the same thing. Broadly speaking, meaning consists in inserting small parts into a larger, integrated context, while information is the opposite. Information is ideally communicated as a binary code, while meaning is communicated more symbolically. Information is handled or 'processed', while meaning is interpreted.[64] Now is it obvious that we cannot simply choose to do without information in favour of meaning, for if one is to be reasonably functional in today's world, one has to be able to deal critically with an abundance of information communicated via many different links. Anyone insisting on gleaning all experiences personally would definitely come a cropper. The problem is that modern technology more and more makes us passive observers and consumers, and less and less active players. This gives us a meaning deficit.

It is not all that easy to give an account of what I mean by 'meaning' here. In philosophical semantics there are a host of different theories about meaning that – especially in continuation of the works of Gottlob Frege – seek to provide an account of meaning in terms of linguistic expression. But the concept of meaning I am referring to has a further perspective, because we are talking about a meaning that is inextricably linked to being a meaning for *someone*. Peter Wessel Zapffe attempted to articulate a concept of meaning:

> That an action or some other fragment of life has meaning means that it gives us a quite specific feeling that is not easy to translate into thought. It would have to be something like the action having a good enough intention, so that when the intention is fulfilled, the action is 'justified', settled, confirmed – and the subject calms down.[65]

This is an odd sort of definition, but it contains the vital element – that this meaning is related to a person's goal-oriented use of the world. At this point, I would just mention that an important difference between Zapffe's and my concept of meaning is that he justifies it biologically, while I justify it more historically. As Zapffe also indicates, these actions also point forward to something more – to life as a whole. I do not intend to pursue Zapffe's considerations here, but will content myself with stating that the meaning we are looking for – or even demand – is ultimately an existential or metaphysical meaning.[66] This existential meaning can be sought in various ways and exists in various forms. It can be conceived as something already given in which one can participate (e.g. in a religious community) or as something that has to be realized (e.g. a classless society). It is conceived as something collective or something individual. I would also assert that the conception of meaning that is particularly prevalent in the West from Romanticism onwards is that which conceives existential meaning as an individual meaning that has to be realized. It is this meaning that I refer to as a *personal meaning*, but I could also call it the *Romantic meaning*.

Human beings are addicted to meaning. We all have a great problem: Our lives must have some sort of content. We cannot bear to live our lives without some sort of content that we can see as constituting a meaning. Meaninglessness is boring. And boredom can be described metaphorically as a meaning withdrawal. Boredom can be understood as a discomfort which communicates that the need for meaning is not being satisfied. In order to remove this discomfort, we attack the symptoms rather than the disease itself, and search for all sorts of meaning-surrogates.

A society that functions well promotes man's ability to find meaning in the world; one that functions badly does not. In premodern societies there is usually a collective meaning that is sufficient.[67] For us 'Romantics', things are more problematic, for even though we often embrace collectivist modes of thought, such as nationalism, they always ultimately appear to be sadly insufficient. Of course, there is still meaning, but there seems to be less of it. Information, on the other hand, there is plenty of. Modern media have made an enormous search for knowledge possible – something that undeniably has positive aspects, but by far the most of it is irrelevant noise. If, on the other hand, we choose to use the word 'meaning' in a broad sense, there is no lack of meaning in the world – there is a superabundance. We positively wade through meaning. But this meaning is not the meaning we are looking for. The emptiness of time in boredom is not an emptiness of action, for there is always *something* in this time, even if it is only the sight of paint drying. The emptiness of time is an emptiness of meaning.

Horkheimer and Adorno made a point that is close to Benjamin's assertion concerning the growth of information. In continuation of Kant's theory of interpretation, schematism, they wrote that

The contribution that Kantian schematism still expected of the subjects – relating in advance the sensory diversity to the underlying concepts – was taken from them by industry. It carries out schematism like a service for the customer . . . For the consumer there is nothing left to classify that has not already been anticipated in production's own schematism.[68]

I believe that boredom is the result of a lack of personal meaning, and that this to a great extent is due precisely to the fact that all objects and actions come to us fully coded, while we – as the descendants of Romanticism – insist on a *personal* meaning. As Rilke wrote in the first of his *Duino*

Elegies, we are not as a matter of course completely at home in the interpreted world. Man is a world-forming being, a being that actively constitutes his own world, but when everything is always already fully coded, the active constituting of the world is made superfluous, and we lose friction in relation to the world. We Romantics need a meaning that we ourselves realize – and the person who is preoccupied with self-realization inevitably has a meaning problem. There is no *one* collective meaning in life any more, a meaning that it is up to the individual to participate in. Nor is it that easy to find one's own meaning in life, either. The meaning that most people embrace is self-realization as such, but it is not obvious what *type* of self is to be realized, nor what should possibly result from it. The person who is certain as regards himself will not ask the question as to who he is. Only a problematic self feels the need for realization.

Boredom presupposes subjectivity, i.e., self-awareness. Subjectivity is a necessary but not a sufficient condition for boredom. To be able to be bored the subject must be able to perceive himself as an individual that can enter into various meaning contexts, and this subject demands meaning of the world and himself. Without such a demand for meaning there would be no boredom. Animals can be understimulated, but hardly bored.[69] As Robert Nisbet has argued:

> Man is apparently unique in his capacity for boredom. We share with all forms of life periodic apathy, but apathy and boredom are different . . . Boredom is much farther up the scale of afflictions than is apathy, and it is probably only a nervous system as highly developed as man's that is even capable of boredom. And within the human species, a level of mentality at least 'normal' appears to be a requirement. The moron may know apathy but not boredom.[70]

Goethe remarked somewhere that monkeys would be worth considering as humans if they were capable of being bored – and he may well be right about that. At the same time, boredom is inhuman because it robs human life of meaning, or possibly it is an expression of the fact that such a meaning is absent.

With Romanticism there comes a strong focusing on a self that is constantly in danger of acquiring a meaning deficiency. The growth of boredom is linked to the growth of nihilism, but the problem-history of nihilism, and possibly its end, is a terribly complex issue of its own and will not be dealt with here to any great extent. Boredom and nihilism converge in the death of God. The first important use of the concept of nihilism in philosophy is in F. H. Jacobi's 'Brief an Fichte' (1799).[71] One of the main points made by Jacobi in this open letter is that man has chosen between God and nothingness, and by choosing nothingness man makes himself a god. This logic is later reiterated, but this time in the affirmative, by Kirilov in Dostoevsky's *The Possessed*: 'If God does not exist, then I become God.'[72] As we know, we chose nothingness, although the word 'chose' is probably misleading here – it *happened*. But man did not fulfil the role of a god all that successfully. Kirilov also claims that in the absence of God 'I am obliged to express my own wilfulness.' In the absence of God man assumed the role of gravitational centre for meaning – but this was a role he managed to fill only to a small extent.

BOREDOM, WORK AND LEISURE

Boredom is connected to reflection, and in all reflection there is a tendency towards a loss of world. Reflection decreases via diversions, but this will always be a passing phenomenon. Work is often less boring than diversions are, but the person who advocates work as a cure for boredom is confusing a temporary removal of the symptoms with curing a disease. And there is no escaping the fact that many forms of work are deadly boring. Work is often onerous, often without potential to promote any meaning in life. The answer to the question as to why people get bored does not lie in work or leisure on their own. One can have a lot of leisure without being noticeably bored, and one can have only a little leisure and be bored to death. The fact that by increasing profits from production in modern industry it has been possible to shorten working hours and prolong leisure does not necessarily lead to any improvement in the quality of life. Boredom is not a question of idleness but of *meaning*.

In his *Book of Disquiet* Fernando Pessoa puts it this way:

It is said that tedium is a disease of the idle, or that it attacks only those who have nothing to do. But this ailment of the soul is in fact more subtle: it attacks people who are predisposed to it, and those who work or who pretend they work (which in this case comes down to the same thing) areless apt to be spared than the truly idle.

Nothing is worse than the contrast between the natural splendour of the inner life, with its natural Indias and its unexplored lands, and the squalor (even when it's not really squalid) of life's daily routine. And tedium is more oppressive when there's not the excuse of idleness. The tedium of those who strive hard is the worst of all.

Tedium is not the disease of being bored because there's nothing to do, but the more serious disease of feeling that there's nothing worth doing. This means that the more there is to do, the more tedium one will feel.

How often, when I look up from the ledger where I enter accounts, my head is devoid of the whole world! I'd be better off remaining idle, doing nothing and having nothing to do, because that tedium, though real enough,

I could at least enjoy. In my present tedium there is no rest, no nobility, and no well-being against which to feel unwell: there's a vast effacement of every act I do, rather than a potential weariness from acts I'll never do.[73]

Pessoa is right in saying that hard work is often just as boring as idleness. I have personally never been so bored as when I was in the process of completing a large dissertation after several years of work. The work bored me so much that I had to mobilize all my will in order to continue, and all that I felt in doing so was a tremendous tiredness. The work seemed to me to be completely meaningless, and I completed it almost like an automaton. When I handed in the dissertation I felt an enormous sense of relief, and thought that I would find life more meaningful again, now that I could be idle. And so I did for a few weeks, but then things returned to the same as before.

Leisure is in itself no more meaningful than work, and the more basic question is *how* one chooses to be idle. Very few of us indeed have any reason to live a life of total idleness, and alternate between work and free time. We start by working the whole day, then watch TV all evening before sleeping all night. This is a fairly common life-pattern. Adorno linked boredom to alienation at work, where free time corresponds to the absence of self-determination in the production process.[74] Free time is a time where you are free, or can be free. What sort of freedom are we talking about? A freedom from work? In that case, it is work that provides a negative definition of freedom. Are we freer in our free time than during our time at work? We undeniably have a slightly different role, for while we are producers in our working hours, we are mainly consumers in our free time. However, one is not necessarily more free in the one role than in the other, and the one role is not necessarily more meaningful than the other. As mentioned, boredom is not a question of work or freedom but of meaning.

Work that does not give very much meaning in life is followed by free time that gives just as little meaning in life. Why does work not give any real meaning? Naturally, it might be tempting simply to refer to alienation, but I prefer instead to talk about an indifference, for I do not believe that the concept of alienation is all that applicable any more. I return to this in the last part of my book. In Milan Kundera's *Identity*, one of the characters, Jean-Marc, says:

> I'd say that the quantity of boredom, if boredom is measurable, is much greater today than it was. Because the old occupations, at least most of them, were unthinkable without a passionate involvement: the peasants in love with their land; my grandfather, the magician of beautiful tables; shoemakers who knew every villager's feet by heart; the woodsmen; the gardeners; probably even the soldiers killed with passion back then. The meaning of life wasn't an issue; it was there with them, quite naturally, in their workshops, in their fields. Each occupation had created its own mentality, its own way of being. A doctor would think differently from a peasant, a soldier would behave in a different way from a teacher. Today we're all alike, all of us bound together by our shared apathy towards our work. That very apathy has become a passion. The one great collective passion of our time.[75]

Kundera is considerably romanticizing the past here, but, even so, I believe has got hold of something essential in drawing attention to the levelling out of differences and the resulting indifference. This also indicates why work in itself can no longer be considered as some sort of list of answers. Work is no longer part of some larger context of meaning that gives it meaning. To the extent that work could possibly be a cure for boredom today, it would be so in the same way as a fix or a bottle – as an attempt to escape from time itself.

Is modern life first and foremost an attempt to escape from boredom? Boredom enforces a movement towards transcending barriers, which in Baudelaire is mainly identified with perversities and the *new*. And *Les Fleurs du mal* ends in 'Le Voyage', where death is the only new thing that remains:

> *Ô Mort, vieux capitaine, il est temps! levons l'ancre!*
> *Ce pays nous ennuie, ô Mort! Appareillons!*
> *Si le ciel et la mer sont noirs comme de l'encre,*
> *Nos cœurs que tu connais sont remplis de rayons!*
>
> *Verse-nous ton poison pour qu'il nous réconforte!*
> *Nous voulons, tant ce feu nous brûle le cerveau,*
> *Plonger au fond du gouffre, Enfer ou Ciel, qu'importe?*
> *Au fond de l'Inconnu pour trouver du nouveau!*

> O Death, old captain, the time has come! Let's raise the
>   anchor!
> This country wearies us, O Death! We'll hoist the sail!
> Even if both heaven and sea are inky black,
> Our hearts, how well you know, are filled with light.
>
> So, pour out your poison, it will comfort us!
> As this fire boils our brains, we want to plumb
> The abyss's depths – who cares if it's heaven or hell? –
> To find, in the deep vaults of the unknown, the *new*! [76]

As Walter Benjamin stated in *Zentralpark*: 'For people as they are today there is only one thing that is radically new – and it is always the same: death.' [77]

Events, no matter how unimportant they may be, take place surrounded by camera lenses and microphones, and they can be blown up to enormous proportions. Everything is potentially visible – nothing is hidden. We can speak of a pan-trans-parency, where everything is transparent. The transparency and the packaged interpretations of the world are interrelated. The trans-parency is precisely not immediate, always mediat-ed, as the world is seen through something, i.e., an already existing interpretation that empties it of secrets. The world becomes boring when everything is transparent. That is why some people hanker for what is dangerous and shocking. They have replaced the non-transparent by the extreme. That is probably why many are so obsessed with the 'street violence' and 'blind violence' that the tabloid press thrives on reporting. How boring life would be without violence!

This is well expressed in a poem written by a former skin-head:

> Everywhere they are waiting, In silence.
> In boredom. Staring into space.
> Reflecting on nothing, or on violence . . .
> Then suddenly it happens. A motor-cycle
> Explodes outside, a cup smashes.
> They are on their feet, identified
> At last as living creatures,
> The universal silence is shattered,
> The law is overthrown, chaos
> Has come again.[78]

The chaos and violence is what moves one from boredom to life, awakening oneself. Providing life with some sort of meaning. We have an aesthetic attitude towards violence, and this aesthetic was clearly apparent in the anti-aesthetic of modernism, with its focus on the shocking and the hideous. In addition, we have a moral attitude towards violence, which we want to see reduced – but I do not know if the moral regard necessarily outweighs the aesthetic one. The conflict of values in modern societies does not only occur between dissimilar social groups – it is perhaps just as much a question of conflicts within the individual subjects, who participate in different spheres of values, as, for example, a moral and an aesthetic sphere. Just as rarely as the conflicts between the various groups can be resolved by referring to a neutral, higher instance can the conflicts within the individual subjects be resolved in such a way.

Violence is 'interesting', no matter what. Towards the end of his essay 'The Work of Art in the Age of Mechanical Reproduction' Benjamin observed that 'Mankind . . . , which in Homer's time was an object of contemplation for the Olympian gods, now is one for itself. Its self-alienation has reached such a degree that it can experience its own destruction as an aesthetic pleasure of the first order.' [79] Boredom leads to most things appearing to be a tempting alternative, and it might seem as if what we really need is a fresh war or a major catastrophe. Nisbet believes that boredom can be catastrophic: 'Boredom may become Western man's greatest source of unhappiness. Catastrophe alone would appear to be the surest and, in today's world, the most likely of liberations from boredom.' [80] The problem is that there is no particular reason to believe that those who survive after a catastrophe will be spared boredom. But for the person who is outside the catastrophe, the world stricken by a catastrophe will seem to be an interesting alternative to boredom. In *The Diary of a Country Priest*, Georges Bernanos prophesises that boredom will be the most obvious cause of the destruction of mankind:

> For if the human race disappears, it will be out of ennui and boredom. Mankind will gradually be consumed like a beam is eaten up by an invisible fungus . . . Look at these world wars, for example, which apparently bear witness to a violent vitality in man but which actually prove its growing lethargy. It will end with vast numbers being led to the slaughter at certain times.[81]

Boredom gives a sort of pallid foretaste of death, and one could imagine that violent actual death would be preferable, that one would prefer the world to end with a bang rather than with a miserable little whimper. Nietzsche has also mentioned the pleasure and sublimity associated with a world meeting its doom.[82]

What boredom seems to have is that it provides some sort of perspective on existence, where one realizes that one is completely insignificant in such a vast context. Joseph Brodsky reckons that 'boredom speaks today's language, and it will teach you your life's most important lesson . . . that you are completely insignificant.'[83] As a finite being, one is surrounded by an infinity of a time that is devoid of content. The experiencing of time changes, with the past and future disappearing and everything becoming a merciless now. Talking Heads sing 'Heaven is a place where nothing ever happens.' In that respect, boredom seems heavenly. It is as if infinity has moved into this world from the beyond. But this infinity, or monotony, is different from the one described by mystics. Simone Weil elaborates on the difference between the two:

> Sameness is both the most beautiful and repulsive thing that exists. The most beautiful if it reflects eternity. The ugliest if it is a sign of something endless and unchangeable. Conquered time or infertile time. The symbol of beautiful sameness is the circle. The symbol of cruel sameness is the ticking of a pendulum.[84]

Time in boredom is not something that has been conquered: time is imprisoning. Boredom is related to death, but it is a paradoxical relationship because profound boredom is like some sort of death, while death assumes the form of the only state possible – a total break with boredom. Boredom has to do with finitude and nothingness. It is a death within life, a non-life. In the in-humanity of boredom we gain a perspective on our own humanity.

TYPOLOGIES OF BOREDOM

Much boredom derives from repetition. I am often bored, for example, when I go to museums and galleries and only find pale imitations of works I have seen already far too many times. I am bored when I hear a lecture for the fourth time, and I am bored when *I* give a lecture for the fourth time.

It can happen that one accepts assignments one is not really qualified for, simply because one will surely learn something new in the process. Seen thus, boredom is a positive source of human development, though not necessarily of progress. We can be bored in many ways. We can be bored with objects and people, we can be bored with ourselves. But an anonymous form of boredom also exists where nothing in particular bores us. *One* feels bored, for boredom does not have any content that can make it *mine*. In this last instance, it would perhaps be more correct to say, in true Heidegger style, that boredom is bored.

There are many different typologies of boredom. Milan Kundera, for example, lists three: passive boredom, as when one yawns disinterestedly; active boredom, as when one devotes oneself to a hobby; and rebellious boredom, as when one – as a young man, say – smashes shop windows.[85] I don't feel this typology is particularly illuminating. It does nothing more than emphasise that one can react passively or actively, and it fails to distinguish qualitatively between various forms of boredom.

I prefer Martin Doehlemann's typology, which distinguishes between four types of boredom: situative boredom, as when one is waiting for someone, is listening to a lecture or taking the train; the boredom of satiety, when one gets too much of the same thing and everything becomes banal; existential boredom, where the soul is without content and the world is in neutral; and creative boredom, which is not so much characterized by its content as its result: that one is forced to do something new.[86] These four overlap, but there are clear distinctions.

Flaubert distinguished between 'common boredom' (*ennui commun*) and 'modern boredom' (*ennui moderne*),[87] which, broadly speaking, corresponds to our distinction between situative and existential boredom. It is, however, not altogether easy to determine the boredom that afflicts the characters in Flaubert's novels in relation to this division. Is the boredom that afflicts Bouvard and Pécuchet 'common' or 'modern'? It is 'common' in the sense that they are bored when prevented from doing something concrete, i.e., devoting themselves to their insane studies of everything between heaven and earth, but it is more 'modern' in the sense that it affects their existence as a whole.[88] Nevertheless, I am inclined to say that both of them suffer from 'common' boredom. The boredom experienced by Emma Bovary, on the other hand, seems to be more of the 'modern' kind, even though her boredom is also object-related via the imaginary object she attempts to realize sexually. A way of distinguishing between situative and existential boredom would be to say that while situative boredom contains a longing for something that is desired, existential boredom contains a longing for any desire at all.

We can note the fact that situative and existential boredom have different symbolic modes of expression, or rather: While situative boredom is expressed via yawning, wriggling in one's chair, stretching out one's arms and legs, etc., profound existential boredom is more of less devoid of expression. While the body language of situative boredom seems to signal that one can cast off this yoke, squirm free and move on, it is as if the lack of expression in existential boredom implies that it cannot be overcome by any act of will. To the extent that there is a clear form of expression for profound boredom, it is via behaviour that is radical and breaks new ground, negatively indicating boredom as its prerequisite. It actually helps to wriggle in one's chair during a lecture or a meeting, and it helps to go on a trip. One gains temporary relief from boredom. As the narrator says in Alberto Moravia's novel *La Noia*, comparing his own boredom with that which plagued his father:

> Father had indeed suffered from boredom, he too, but for him this suffering had been acted out in a happy vagabond-like existence in various regions. His boredom, in other words, was a vulgar boredom, as one normally understands the term, a boredom that does not require anything else to be assuaged than new, unusual experiences.[89]

The narrator himself, on the other hand, suffers from a boredom that goes much deeper, and a more profound form of boredom obviously needs a more desperate remedy, i.e. behaviour that is more radical and transfrontier. Georges Bataille has commented thus: 'There is no feeling that is more exhilarating than the awareness of the emptiness that surrounds us. This does not at all mean that we do not experience an emptiness inside ourselves, on the contrary: but we overcome this feeling and enter into an awareness of the transgression.'[90] The awareness of an emptiness is the prerequisite for crossing frontiers, but, as we shall see, crossing frontiers does not help in the long run, for how is one to escape from a *world* that is boring? [91]

Schopenhauer described this boredom as a 'tame longing without any particular object'.[92] In profound boredom one loses the capacity to find any object whatsoever for one's desire. The world has withered and died. Kafka complained in his diary that he experienced something that was 'As if everything I owned had left me, and as if it would scarcely be sufficient if all of it returned.' [93] In Moravia's *La Noia*, it is said that boredom is 'like a disease of the things themselves, a disease that leads to all vitality withering and dying, almost quite suddenly vanishing.' [94] Boredom is like a 'fog'.[95] We also find this expression in Heidegger, who refers to profound boredom as a 'silent fog' that draws together all things and people, including even itself, into a strange indifference.[96] Garborg also has an apt description: 'I can't find any better way of referring to it than a mental cold – a cold that has gone to the mind.'[97] The descriptions vary, from ascribing the numbness and emptiness to the ego and to the world, presumably because it belongs to both spheres. Freud claims that 'in mourning it is the world that has become poor and empty; in melancholia it is the ego itself.'[98] As Adam Phillips points out in commenting on this passage: 'And in boredom, we might add, it is both.'[99] It is impossible to say if something is boring because one happens to be in a state of boredom or whether one begins to feel bored because the world is bored. It is impossible to make any clear distinction between the respective contributions made by the subject and object to boredom, because the emptiness of the subject and object is so interwoven. Fernando Pessoa describes being affected by boredom as like having the drawbridge over the moat round the castle of our soul suddenly raised, so that there is no longer any connection between the castle and the surrounding land. Further:

> I observe myself. I'm my own spectator. My sensations pass, like external things, before I don't know what gaze of mine. I bore myself no matter what I do. All things, down to their roots in mystery, have the colour of my boredom.[100]

Dostoevsky talks at one point about boredom as being a

'bestial and indefinable affliction'.[101] This apparently vague description is actually very precise. Boredom is practically indefinable because it lacks the positiveness that is typical of most other phenomena. It is basically to be understand as an absence – an absence of personal meaning. And, as I shall say later in my discussion of Heidegger's analysis of boredom, this loss of meaning reduces human life to something analogous to an existence that is purely animal.

BOREDOM AND NOVELTY

Martin Doehlemann has claimed that boredom is characterized by a dearth of experiences.[102] This applies to situative boredom, where it is something specific, or the lack of something specific, that bores one. Although it ought to be clarified that both a surplus *and* a deficit of experiences can lead to boredom.[103] Existential boredom, on the other hand, must fundamentally be understood on the basis of a concept of a *dearth of accumulated experience.* The problem is that we try to get beyond this boredom by piling on increasingly new and more potent sensations and impressions, instead of allowing ourselves time to accumulate experience. It is as if we believe that we will manage to establish a substantial self, free of boredom, if only we manage to fill it with a sufficient number of impulses. When one throws oneself at everything that is new, it is with a hope that the new will be able to have an individualizing function and supply life with a personal meaning; but everything new soon becomes old, and the promise of personal meaning is not always fulfilled – at least, not more than just for the time being. The new always quickly turns into routine, and then comes boredom with the new that is always the same, boredom at discovering that everything is intolerably identical behind the false differences between objects and thoughts',[104] as Pessoa expresses it, because the fashionable always reveals itself as the 'same old thing in a brand new drag', as David Bowie sings in *Teenage Wildlife*.

Modernity has had fashion as a principle, and fashion, as Benjamin said, is 'the eternal recurrence of the *new*'.[105] Fashion is a tremendously important phenomenon.[106] In a world with fashion as a principle we get more stimuli but also more boredom, more emancipation and corresponding slavery, more individuality and more abstract impersonality. The only individuality in fashion is one that consists in out-bidding the others, but for precisely this reason one ends up being completely controlled by them. As Georg Simmel pointed out a century ago, it is actually the case that the leader ends up by being led.[107] And the person who decides to adopt a negative attitude towards fashion by consciously deviating from it – for example, by being unmodern – is just as bound by fashion, because the personal style is simply defined as a negation of fashion.

A fashion object does not strictly speaking need to have any quality except that of being new. *Quality* comes from the Latin *qualitas*, which perhaps can be translated as nature, or character.[108] The quality of an object has to do with what sort of a thing it is, and an object without quality is an object without identity. For earlier societies, things were bearers of continuity and stability, but this is the diametric opposite of the principle of fashion. The principle of fashion is to create an ever more rapid tempo, to make an object superfluous as soon as possible, so as to be able to move on to a new one. Kant was probably right in saying that it is better to be an idiot of fashion than just an idiot,[109] but every idiot of fashion will, sooner of later, be let down. And fashion is impersonal by nature. So it cannot supply us with the personal meaning we are striving for.

When everything becomes interchangeable and, in terms of value, non-different (read: indifferent), genuine preferences become impossible, and we end up either in total randomness or in a total paralysis of action. Remember Buridan's ass, which starves to death because it cannot cope with having to choose between two identical heaps of food? Rational decisions presuppose preferences, and preferences presuppose differences. The novel that best presents this decadent mania of distinction is probably J.-K. Huysmans' *A Rebours* (1884). In it the Count of Esseintes, ill with boredom, can only bring content into his life by hyper-subtle distinctions and by making well-staged surroundings artificial.[110] In Bret Easton Ellis's *American Psycho*, the difference between, for example, two types of mineral water or two recordings of *Les Misérables* becomes more important than anything else in life. We distinguish one brand of clothing from another, one malt whisky from another, one sexual practice from another. We are desperate in our search for differences. Fortunately, or regrettably, the advertising industry is there to save us with new distinctions. Advertising is essentially nothing more than creating qualitative differences where there are none. Most products of a certain type (clothing, cars, etc.) are almost completely identical and therefore without *qualitas*, without their own nature. For that reason, it becomes even more important to create a difference that can distinguish products from one another. It is the actual distinction that is important, not its content, for by establishing such differences we hope to maintain a belief that the world still has qualities.

We become major consumers of new things and new people in order to break the monotony of things being the same. Somewhat cryptically, Roland Barthes wrote that 'Boredom is not far removed from desire: it is desire seen from the shores of pleasure.'[111] I think that pleasure should be understood here as meaning 'the same', while desire should be understood as that which goes beyond 'the same', that which is 'outside' – transcendence. Boredom is immanence in its purest form. The antidote must apparently be transcendence. But how can transcendence be possible within an immanence – and immanence that consists of nothing? For a transcendence has to be a something. How do we escape from nothing to something? And is boredom in its most profound form not characterized by our becoming indifferent as to whether anything exists?[112] Jean Baudrillard claims that while the traditional philosophical question used to be 'Why is there anything at all, rather than nothing?', the real question today is 'Why is there just nothing, rather than something?'[113] These are questions that spring from a profound boredom. And in this boredom all of reality is at stake.

Fernando Pessoa describes this emptiness beautifully:

Everything is emptiness, even the idea of emptiness. Everything is said in a language that is incomprehensible to us, a stream of syllables that do not re-echo in our understanding. Life is empty, the soul is empty, the world is empty. All the gods die a death that is greater than death itself. Everything is emptier than emptiness. Everything is a chaos of nothing.

When I think like that, and look around me in the hope that reality must surely quench my thirst, I see expressionless gestures. Stones, bodies, thoughts – everything is dead. All movement has come to a standstill, and everything stands still in the same way. Nothing says anything to me. Nothing is known, though not because I find it strange but because I do not know what it is. The world has been lost. And in the depths of my soul – which is the only thing that is real at this moment – there is a sharp, invisible pain, a sadness that resembles the sound it makes, like tears in a dark room.[114]

TWO

Stories of Boredom

This chapter sketches out the history of our subject from the medieval *acedia* (or *accidia*) via the boredom of the Romantic era through to Andy Warhol's post-Romantic boredom.[1] The intention is for this chapter to have a relevance over and above the purely historical, for it describes various boredom strategies that are topical today. I also wish to indicate why I view most of these strategies as being mistaken – something I will return to in chapter Four.

ACEDIA: PRE-MODERN BOREDOM

We saw earlier that Kierkegaard described boredom as 'the root of all evil'. In doing so, he was in accordance with medieval theology, where *acedia* was considered a particularly grievous sin, since all other sins sprang from it. The concept of *acedia* has a complicated history that stretches for over a millennium, from its beginnings in antiquity through to the late-medieval period, at which time it was ousted by the new concept of melancholy.[2] The surviving accounts of *acedia*, mainly by Christian thinkers in late antiquity and the Middle Ages, correspond to a great extent to what we know as boredom, with indifference and idleness as important characteristics. A crucial difference is that *acedia* is first and foremost a moral concept, whereas 'boredom', in the normal sense of the word, more describes a psychological state. Another difference is that *acedia* was for the few, whereas boredom afflicts the masses.

There are words in ancient Greek for idleness (e.g., *skholé, álys* and *argós*) and for a kind of satiety or blasé state of mind (e.g., *kóros*), but hardly anything that wholly corresponds to our concept of boredom. The closest is probably *akedía*, which is made up of *kedos*, which means to care about, and a negative prefix. The concept, however, plays only a minor role in early Greek thought, where it described a state of disintegration that could manifest itself as stupor and lack of participation. It is not until the fourth century AD, with the Christian Early Fathers in the deserts beyond Alexandria, that the term acquires a more technical meaning, now describing a state of satiety with life, or tiredness. Evagrius Ponticus (*c.* 345–399) conceives *acedia* as being demonic. The midday demon (*daemon meridianus*) is the most cunning of all demons, attacking the monk in the middle of the day, in broad daylight, causing the sun to seem to be standing utterly still in the sky. Things intrude in this state, but appear to be completely de-animated. The demon causes him to detest the place where he finds himself – and even life itself. It causes the monk to remember the life he lived before becoming a monk, with all its attractions, tempting him to give up a life devoted to God. According to Evagrius, the person who can withstand *acedia*, through stamina and patience, will also be able to withstand all other sins. And what follows is *joy*. The person who is full of joy does not sin, which is why overcoming *acedia* can lead to virtue.

For Johannes Cassian (*c.* 360–432), the word *acedia* is no longer to be considered to be something demonic; rather, it is a hermitic sub-species of common sadness. He emphasises that *acedia* leads to other sins, a claim that was keenly debated in the Middle Ages. The prominent position of *acedia* among the sins is not only due to the fact that other sins flow from it but that it contained a rejection of – or rather detestation of – God and his Creation. *Acedia* is the diametric opposite of the joy one ought to feel towards God and his works. It prevents man's redemption and pitches him into eternal perdition.

That things did not go too well for those who succumbed to *acedia* is seen in Dante's *Commedia* (*c.* 1300). Dante placed his *accidiosi* in deep mire, where they whine over their punishment for the bad humour they abandoned themselves to, when they should have rejoiced in the sunshine:

> Fix'd in the slime they say: 'Sad once were we
> In the sweet air made gladsome by the sun,
> Carrying a foul and lazy mist within:
> Now in these murky settlings are we sad.'
> Such dolorous strain they gurgle in their throats.
> But word distinct can utter none.[3]

In the Renaissance, the concept of *acedia* was superseded by that of melancholy. That was not least due to the more naturalistic perspective then being placed on the world. *Acedia* differed from melancholy by being linked to the soul, whereas melancholy was normally linked to the body. Melancholy becomes 'natural', while *acedia* had stronger moral implications. It is also worth noting that while melancholy is an ambiguous concept that includes both illness and wisdom, *acedia* remains a purely negative concept. While melancholy can contain its own cure, the cure for *acedia* always lies outside the state itself – for example, in God or in work.

After the fourteenth century *acedia* was considered less as a sin and more as an illness, but the moral aspects of *acedia* have, to a certain extent, been taken over by boredom. We often have a censorious attitude towards boredom – both in ourselves and in others. We often consider it to spring from a fundamental defect of character, or, if we are to be more 'objective', as a personality disorder. This is also evident in today's psychological investigations. Such an approach is unsatisfactory because it overlooks the possibility that the outside world – rather than the person – is the problem, or disallows that the world plays any decisive role at all. Boredom is not just a phenomenon that afflicts individuals; it is, to just as great an extent, a social and cultural phenomenon.

FROM PASCAL TO NIETZSCHE

The most prominent early theoretician of boredom is Pascal. He also forms a suitable transition from *acedia* to boredom since he so closely links boredom to a theological complex of problems. At the same time, he is difficult to make out, for his *Thoughts* seem in many ways simply too modern to have been written in the seventeenth century. He does, however, follow what was written in Ecclesiastes, i.e., that all the godlessness men display is meaningless, empty vanity.

For Pascal, man is doomed to boredom without God: 'One needs no great sublimity of soul to realize that in this life there is no true and solid satisfaction.'[4] In the absence of a relationship to God we turn to pleasures in order to forget our miserable state, but in actual fact this only has a more destructive effect, because these lead us even further away from the Creator:

> The only thing that consoles us for our miseries is diversion. And yet it is the greatest of our miseries. For it is that above all which prevents us thinking about ourselves and leads us imperceptibly to destruction. But for that we should be bored, and boredom would drive us imperceptibly to our death.[5]

Pascal actually sums up all the various human doings under

the umbrella concept 'diversion'.[6] One's whole life becomes a flight from life, which is fundamentally a boring nothingness without God:

> Man finds nothing so intolerable as to be in a state of complete rest, without passions, without occupation, without diversion, without effort. Then he feels his nullity, loneliness, inadequacy, dependence, helplessness, emptiness. And at once there wells up from the depths of his soul boredom, gloom, depression, chagrin, resentment, despair.[7]

Diversion might seem to be preferable to the misery of life, because it can create an illusion of happiness – at least for a while. The attempt to escape from boredom via diversions is synonymous with a flight from reality, a flight from the nothing that the individual human being is. Boredom does not have any important societal dimension in Pascal; it should rather be seen as an essential characteristic of man as such. Without God, man is nothing, and boredom is the awareness of this nothingness. Those who encounter their own boredom therefore have far greater self-perception than those who only seek diversions. In boredom, man is completely left to himself, but this is being left to a nothingness, because there does not exist any relationship to anything else. For that reason, suffering is perhaps preferable in a certain sense to boredom, because suffering is at least *something*. But since we are so privileged that we do not need to abandon ourselves to suffering, we might just as well give ourselves up to diversions. There, however, stands boredom once more as an unavoidable fact. For Pascal, there is only one lasting cure.

Let us move on to a thinker who – despite the fact that he himself was a believer – has done more than anyone else to dethrone God, namely Kant. It is amazing to find such perceptive descriptions of boredom in Kant, since he only has a concept of a time of experience and no well-developed conception of the experiencing of time. But all great philosophers have brilliant thoughts that do not really have any logical place in their system. The best observations concerning boredom in Kant are found in a lecture on ethics, 'On the Duties in Life in Relation to States'.

It is remarkable that Kant deals with boredom within the context of moral philosophy, and that he also talks about duties as a way of promoting certain states. In that sense, he is perpetuating the *acedia* tradition. However, I intend to focus on the more general anthropological aspects here. For Kant, boredom is linked to cultural development. While individual children of nature live in a state of alternation between needs and the satisfying of those needs, cultivated individuals are driven towards boredom via a desire to experience constantly *new* forms of pleasure.[8] In boredom, man feels a detestation or nausea at his own existence.[9] It is a dread of the void, *horror vacui*, that gives a foretaste of a 'slow death'.[10] The more one is aware of time, the emptier it feels.[11] The only cure is work, not pleasures.[12] 'Man is the only animal that has to work.'[13] The necessity to work should not so much be understood here pragmatically as existentially. Without work we are bored to death, because we cannot cope with living without content for any length of time. Kant claims that 'man *feels* his life through actions and not through enjoyment and that in idleness man feels a 'lack of life.[14] Further:

> The pleasures of life do not fill time but leave it empty. The human mind, however, feels detestation and discomfort in the presence of empty time. Present time can admittedly seem to us to be full, but in our memory it nevertheless appears to be empty, for when time is filled with diversions and the like, it only feels full while it is contemporaneous – in the memory it is empty. For if one

has not done anything in one's life, but simply wasted one's time, and then looks back at one's life, one will be unable to understand how it could come to an end so swiftly.[15]

A good argument against cheap diversions is *memento mori* – remember that you are going to die! I think Adorno is right in saying that death appears to be more frightening the less one has *lived*.[16] In his novel *Relief*, Tor Ulven writes about 'a sorrow, a despair, about what?, you think, and continue: about unlived life; not a grief or fear that after a while you will not be able to experience anything at all any more ... but the nagging feeling of not having experienced anything, of not having had any real life.'[17] Kant points out that life becomes boring precisely for the person that does not *do* anything, and it seems to him 'as if he had never lived at all'.[18] Idleness and boredom lead, then, to a diminution of life. The German for boredom, *Langeweile*, i.e., that which lasts a long time, is partly misleading, because time in boredom can just as well be described as extremely short-lived. It depends on whether one imagines the experiencing of time during actual boredom or in the memory. Because time is not filled out in boredom, the boring span of time appears afterwards to be short, while it is experienced as unbearably long during the actual span of time. Life becomes short when time becomes long. In true, profound boredom, the distinction between the brevity and longevity of time no longer applies. It is as if infinity itself has moved into the world from the beyond – and infinity has no duration.

Kant's reflections on boredom are a clear anticipation of Thomas Mann's theory of boredom, as formulated in Chapter 4 of *The Magic Mountain*, 'Excursion On the Sense of Time':

Many false conceptions are held concerning the nature of tedium. In general it is thought that the interestingness and novelty of the time-content are what 'make the time pass'; that is to say, shorten it; whereas monotony and emptiness check and restrain its flow. This is only true with reservations. Vacuity, monotony, have, indeed, the property of lingering out the moment and the hour and of making them tiresome. But they are capable of contracting and dissipating the larger, the very large time-units, to the point of reducing them to nothing at all. And conversely, a full and interesting content can put wings to the hour and the day; yet it will lend to the general passage of time a weightiness, a breadth and solidity which cause the eventful years to flow far more slowly than those poor, bare, empty ones over which the wind passes and they are gone. Thus what we call tedium is rather an abnormal shortening of the time consequent on monotony. Great spaces of time passed in unbroken uniformity tend to shrink together in a way to make the heart stop beating for fear; when one day is like all the others, then they are all like one; complete uniformity would make the longest life seem short.[19]

Here, Mann gives an excellent phenomenological description of boredom, but the cure he subsequently recommends, namely to frequently change one's habits, is both banal *and* part of the problem. When he says that 'new habits are the only way of keeping our life going', this only helps to maintain the inner logic of boredom. Here, Mann jumps right into the issue that defines Kant's aesthetes.

A few brief remarks concerning the aesthete. Kierkegaard's aesthete in *Either/Or* is a Romantic, trapped in a lifestyle in which he is constantly trying to escape from boredom by outdoing previous pleasures. He only has one ambition in life, to transform the boring into something interesting, thereby re-creating the world in his own image. Kierkegaard describes boredom as a 'demonic pantheism'.[20] The demonic is that which is empty, and the boredom is to be understood as a nothingness that permeates all reality. Kierkegaard regards the feeling of boredom as belonging to the person of rank: 'Those who bore others are the plebeians, the crowd, the endless train of humanity in general; those who bore themselves are the chosen ones, the nobility.' [21] There are probably many people today who would feel flattered by this description, since most people see themselves as being incredibly amusing and interesting, while one is bored out of one's wits by everything else. But perhaps we can read Kierkegaard's remark in a slightly different way. Boredom presupposes an element of self-reflection, or contemplation regarding one's own placement in the world, which calls for time – and this time was normally not something the common people had access to in Kierkegaard's day.

In Schopenhauer, man has the choice, broadly speaking, between suffering and boredom, 'for every human life is thrown back and forth between pain and boredom.' [22] Schopenhauer considers man as a being that incessantly tries to avoid the suffering that is the fundamental condition of life by giving it other forms. But when this reshaping is unsuccessful and suffering simply has to be repressed, life becomes boring. If boredom is successfully broken, suffering will return once more. [23] All life is a striving for existence, but when this has been guaranteed, life no longer knows what to do and lapses into boredom. Therefore, boredom is characteristic of the lives of persons of rank, while need characterizes the lives of the masses. [24] Life for the person of rank becomes primarily a question of disposing of the superabundance of time he has at his disposal. [25] Man knows desire, and the aim of this desire is placed either in nature, society or the power of the imagination. If the aims are not fulfilled, this leads to suffering; and when they are fulfilled, the result is boredom. Because of a lack of satisfaction in the real world, man creates an imaginary world. This is how all religions have come into being – as an attempt to escape boredom. It is also the basis of all artistic activity, and it is only in art – music especially – that man can find bliss.[26] This aesthetic dimension, however, is only accessible to the few. And even for those chosen few, it only represents a few scattered moments in a time that is wretchedly protracted.

Giacomo Leopardi, a strong candidate for history's most melancholy writer, complained incessantly of boredom (*la noia*). Anyone who has visited Leopardi's small home town, Recanati in the Marche, cannot help but understand Leopardi's complaints to some extent. Schopenhauer, by the way, was of the opinion that no one had understood him so well as Leopardi. In a letter of 1819 to his father, Leopardi wrote that he would prefer suffering to this 'deadly boredom' he is suffering from.[27] In *Zibaldone* it is said that the dejection that grows out of boredom is easier to bear than boredom itself.[28] Despair is also preferable to this 'death within life'.[29] At the same time, boredom is the most sublime of all human emotions, because it expresses the fact that the human spirit, in a certain sense, is greater than the entire universe. Boredom is an expression of a profound despair at not finding anything that can satisfy the soul's boundless needs. Further, for Leopardi boredom is reserved for noble souls; 'the mob' can, at best, only suffer from simple idleness.[30]

A corresponding elitism as regards boredom is also found later in Nietzsche.[31] Nietzsche never formulated a 'theory' of boredom, but there are a number of sporadic remarks we can build on. For Nietzsche, boredom is 'the unpleasant "calm" of the soul' that precedes creative acts, and while creative spirits endure boredom, 'lesser natures' flee from it.[32] Nietzsche claimed that 'the machine culture' creates a hopeless boredom that causes us to thirst for changeable idleness.[33] In *Human, All Too Human* (1878), he has this to say:

Ennui and play – Necessity compels us to work, with the product of which the necessity is appeased; the ever new awakening of necessity, however, accustoms us to work. But in the intervals in which necessity is appeased and asleep, as it were, we are attacked by ennui. What is this? In a word it is the habituation to work, which now makes itself felt as a new and additional necessity; it will be all the stronger the more a person has been accustomed to work, perhaps, even, the more a person has suffered from necessities. In order to escape ennui, a man either works beyond the extent of his former necessities, or he invents play, that is to say, work that is only intended to appease the general necessity for work. He who has become satiated with play, and has no new necessities impelling him to work, is sometimes attacked by the longing for a third state, which is related to play as gliding is to dancing, as dancing is to walking, a blessed, tranquil movement; it is the artists' and philosophers' vision of happiness.[34]

The Nietzschean 'I' affirms itself by maintaining its presence in the now as a delight. It is delight that wishes itself for all eternity – 'a profound, profound eternity'.[35] It is an eternity that is circular, not linear. Eternity is *now*. In delight, the moment is wished for so strongly that its recurrence is wished for an endless number of times. Boredom, by being conquered, can lead to delight. To what extent such a delight is attainable for us is another question. Such a delight is superhuman, whereas boredom is human, all too human.

ROMANTIC BOREDOM, FROM *WILLIAM LOVELL* TO *AMERICAN PSYCHO*

The Romantics emphasised boredom as one of the major conditions and inflictions of human life.[36] Novalis, for instance, claimed that nothing was worse.[37] He argued that 'boredom is hunger',[38] but it is not clear precisely what it was he was hungry for. Romantic boredom is characterized by not knowing what one is searching for, other than an unspecified, boundless fullness of life. It is rooted in the search for the infinite, and as Friedrich Schlegel pointed out, 'Whoever desires the infinite is unaware of what he desires.'[39] The Romantic does not know what he is looking for, except that it is to represent some sort of infinite meaning. Without such a 'grand meaning', there is no meaning at all. As Schlegel put it in another fragment: 'Only in relation to the infinite is there meaning and purpose; whatever lacks such a relation is absolutely meaningless and pointless.'[40] However, this very yearning for the infinite, for the absolute, for Meaning, only makes boredom worse.

Of course, Romanticism is far from being an unambiguous concept,[41] so let me clarify things by stating that I am primarily thinking of German Romanticism, which grew out of the thinking of Kant and Fichte from the 1790s onwards, with Jena as its centre. Naturally, I am not of the opinion that a number of brilliant young minds in Jena – Hölderlin, Novalis, Tieck, Schlegel, etc. – were the origins of all later misery. It is rather that here we find an unusually well-defined formulation of a mode of thought that has been widespread over the past 200 to 250 years. We think like Romantics did. Foucault was right to say that Jena was the arena where the fundamental interests in modern Western culture suddenly had their breakthrough.[42] Romanticism is not least a kind of fulfilment of the philosophical individualism that continued to develop beyond the eighteenth century.

Romanticism is aestheticism. This is, of course, no original assertion, but aestheticism becomes extreme subjectivism. All objective criteria disappear, and the subjective, aesthetic experiencing of the world gains unlimited validity. This, however, rapidly ends up marking time. As Hegel points out in his critique of Romantic irony:

Whatever is, is only by the instrumentality of the *ego*, and whatever exists by my instrumentality I can equally well annihilate again.

Now if we stop at these absolutely empty forms which originate from the absoluteness of the abstract *ego*, nothing is treated *in and for itself* and as valuable in itself, but only as produced by the subjectivity of the *ego*. But in that case the *ego* can be lord and master of everything...[43]

The problem is that if it is up to me to ascribe or deny significance and value at will, these things will lose their value and significance, because these are now not inherent in the things themselves and thus become empty. Because there is no substantial distinction between the significant and the insignificant, everything becomes equally interesting and as a result equally boring. Hegel continues:

If the ego remains at this standpoint, everything appears to it as null and vain, except its own subjectivity which therefore becomes hollow and empty and itself mere vanity. But, on the other hand, the ego may, contrariwise, fail to find satisfaction in this self-enjoyment and instead become inadequate to itself, so that it now feels a craving for the solid and the substantial, for specific and essential interests. Out of this comes misfortune, and the contradiction that, on the one hand, the subject does want to penetrate into truth and longs for objectivity, but, on the other hand, cannot renounce his isolation and withdrawal into himself or tear himself free from this unsatisfied abstract inwardness.[44]

This leads to an immense boredom and longing, because the I can no longer manage to fill itself, by itself, at the same time as it insists on itself obtaining the content. In the *Phenomenology of Spirit*, Hegel remarks on 'the frivolity and boredom which unsettle the established order', but only sees this as symptomatic of an uncertainty in the face of a new golden age that is to come.[45] This golden age never came, and it is truer to say that Hegel's *status quo* in many respects is also ours.

Hegel talks about subjectivism as being the most prevalent illness of his age.[46] This subjectivism is connected to Kant's Copernican turn in philosophy. The death of God is not something that happens in Nietzsche. God is already dead in Kant, as God can no longer warrant the objectivity of cognition and the order of the universe. Nor was there any wish for such a guarantee. Man was to stand on his own two feet. What is perhaps the most prominent characteristic of modernity is that man takes over the role that was previously played by God. Qualities that first were ascribed to the things themselves and in the medieval period were increasingly ascribed to God have become aspects of the human subject's constitution of the world. It is clear that Kant is a central figure in this narrative. It is superficial but not unreasonable to say that the Kantian conception of the I is a secularized version of the medieval conception of God. The problem facing this subject is to fill the meaning-void created by the absence of God.

It is worth noting the Romantic reinvestment in the symbol.[47] Where the symbol has an immediate meaning-conveying function, a kind of reality in the form of a sensory presence, there is a gap in allegory between expression and meaning. As far as the symbol is concerned, there is no distinction between the experience and its representation, while allegory extrapolates this distinction. But what should allegory be an allegory of, once God has gone? To once more fill the world with meaning, to be able to experience the world, a return to the symbol became vital for the Romantic. This return, however, was far from successful, for while pre-Romantic symbolism was collective, that of the Romantic era became private. The symbolist's experience of the world is merely his *own* experience, and for the modern, Romantic symbolist it is precisely the *object* that becomes more or less irrelevant.

In Johann Gottlieb Fichte's *Grundzüge des gegenwärtigen Zeitalters* he speculatively outlines a world history with five main epochs, where man first lives in a state of innocence, before falling into a state of decay and finally entering and fulfilling himself in an epoch of reason.[48] Such a philosophy of history is in itself not particularly original or interesting, but Fichte uses this scenario to mount a harsh critique of his own time, which he places in the third epoch. In that age, sinfulness has reached its peak and reason is undergoing its deepest crisis.[49] The crisis is rooted in the individualism that pervades modernity. Subjective freedom in modernity has been separated from the universality of reason, and the ensuing 'naked individualism' finds its expression in hedonism and materialism. Science in such an age is characterized by formalism – an empty formalism without any genuine ideas.[50] In such an age one experiences a great emptiness, 'which reveals itself as an infinite, irremediable and constantly recurring boredom'.[51] In order to avoid this boredom, man reduces everything to entertainment, or flees to various forms of mysticism. According to Fichte, this situation can only be overcome by renouncing individualism and submitting to universal reason. For people of today, however, Fichte's solution is hardly convincing, simply because a belief in universal reason has been seriously undermined and no one knows what such universal reason could possibly be.

In these lectures of 1804, given exactly 20 years after Kant published his essay 'What is Enlightenment?', where Kant encouraged the use of one's *own* reason,[52] Fichte made a diagnosis of modernity that sounds remarkably familiar. He emphasised the boredom of modernity. The paradoxical thing is that the very individualism that Fichte rejected found its most typical expression in the Romanticism that emerged out of Fichte's own *Wissenschaftslehre*. It should, however, be emphasised that it is not Fichte but the Romantics who should be blamed for this paradox by having misread him. Kierkegaard pointed this out in *Concerning the Concept of Irony*:

> The Fichtean principle that the *I* has constitutive *validity*, is the one and only Almighty, was grasped by *Schlegel* and *Tieck*, and from this they operated in the world. This created a double difficulty. First of all, one confused the empirical and finite I with the eternal I; secondly, one confused the metaphysical reality with the historical reality. One thus directly imposed an imperfect *metaphysical* point of view on *reality*.[53]

The relation between modern individualism and boredom is clearly in evidence in the Romantic literature of Fichte's time, and Ludwig Tieck's seldom-read *William Lovell* of 1795–6 is perhaps *the* Romantic novel on boredom.[54] The reason this classic novel is so ignored must be, in large part, because it is so frightfully boring. This opinion was maintained as early as Schlegel, and one can hardly disagree with his claim that in *William Lovell* 'the description of sublime boredom at times shifts into a communication of the thing itself'.[55] Boredom is a challenging artistic topic, with most of the literary presentations of it having a tendency to be just as dull as their subject-matter. Since boredom is a void, it is well-nigh impossible to portray it positively. How does one represent an absence? Samuel Beckett, perhaps, was the first person to achieve this. More of him later. The notion of boredom waylays the reader on the very first page of *William Lovell*, and it maintains a central position throughout. Since the plot is pedestrian and of little interest, I shall focus on the 'philosophy' that is expressed in the novel.

William starts out as a young English dreamer who is sent by his father on a educational journey on the Continent. The outer journey is paralleled by an inner journey. He withdraws into himself and indulges in an uncompromising self-absorption. He perceives this as a liberation, but it is actually an impoverishment. *William Lovell* is not so much a novel of personal development as one of personal disintegration. Everything that is solid melts into air, and the search for a fullness of life is the road to destruction.

In Tieck's novel, existence is a never-ending spiral of boredom: 'I stand here in a joyless world, like a clock ceaselessly describing the same monotonous circular movement.'[56] William demands that the world satisfy him and be interesting, but he can find nothing of interest, and his daily complaint is that he is bored to death; the world as such is a vast prison.[57] He conceives the world and its inhabitants as lacking all originality or capacity to fascinate him. From time to time he reaches a temporary state of euphoria or 'lustful intoxication',[58] but this always rapidly passes away. Man as such no longer 'interests' William, and every single face 'bores him'.[59] William, though, is not the only person who is bored – practically all the characters are. One of William's friends, Karl Wilmont, writes that 'This boredom has already brought more unhappiness into the world than all the passions put together. The soul shrivels up like a dried plum.' [60] Everyone frantically searches for an identity and gets lost in an attempt to transcend boredom, but William goes to greater lengths than the others. All of them have had freedom served on a platter, have been released from the constraints of tradition, but they do not have the faintest idea what they are to do with this freedom, apart from possibly seeking to increase it.

Like numerous fictional cousins – Goethe's Faust, Byron's Manfred and Don Juan, Hölderlin's Hyperion – William *demands* satisfaction. He is therefore caught up in a logic of transgression, since no pleasures can provide anything more than a moment's satisfaction before they must be surpassed by new ones: 'Why can a pleasure never completely fill the heart? What unknowable, sad longing pulls me towards new, unknown pleasures?'[61] Boredom and transgression are intimately connected. It seems as if the only cure for boredom lies in going beyond the self in an increasingly more radical manner because transgression brings the self into contact with something new, something other than the *same* that threatens to drown the self in boredom.

This is a good moment to look at Hölderlin's draft of *Hyperion*, namely *Hyperions Jugend* from 1795, where he says 'We can never deny our urge to expand and liberate ourselves.'[62] Our urge to transgress is ineradicable, and Hölderlin sublimates this yearning for expansion, for reaching a goal that always lies beyond our reach: 'No action, no thought ever reaches as far as you wish. It is man's glory that he is never satisfied.'[63] Our striving for redemption will always be infinitely postponed, and the 'strife' between ourselves and the world will continue and can cease to be only in an infinite perspective. *Hyperion* itself ends with the words 'Nächstens mehr'.[64] Even though the end appears to be harmonious, everything must go on and on, because redemption is always temporary. There are moments, but the moment cannot be halted and gain completion, as time always moves on. Hölderlin and Tieck do not 'cheat' as Goethe does in *Faust*, where he concludes by claiming that striving warrants redemption: 'Wer immer strebend sich bemüht / Den können wir erlösen'. In *Hyperion* and *William Lovell*, striving is no guarantee of redemption. Time always goes on. As a character remarks in Amis's *London Fields*: 'And meanwhile time goes about its immemorial work of making everyone look, and feel, like shit.'[65]

Hölderlin gives a lucid account of the Romantic logic of transgression that springs from a yearning for satisfaction, where the *new* must always be sought in order to avoid the boredom of the same. However, because everything that is sought is only sought because it is new, everything becomes identical by virtue of only being new.[66] William Lovell's friend, Balder, writes: 'The spirit thirsts for the new, one object must replace another . . . and what does it turn out to be except the boring repetition of one and the same thing?'[67] William himself describes how human life passes by in front of his eyes in an eternal state of change, but on closer scrutiny it all proves to be 'the boring, eternal same'.[68]

Even though William wants to transcend, only a 'flat' transcendence is possible because the absolutely transcendent is defined away in advance in favour of seeking the pleasures of the world: 'I attach all my joys and hopes to this life; the hereafter – if it should exist and in whatever form that might be – I will not risk missing any benefits for a dream.'[69] The hereafter is irrelevant. William rejects the existence of any corrective standard outside himself, embracing an out-and-out relativism where everything is determined by one's personal liking.[70] He reduces man to a mere instinctual being and claims that all human actions spring from an urge towards desire.[71] He wishes to be such a being in full. All motivation reveals itself as egoism in the last resort, and 'evil is just a word'.[72] Virtue is mere 'nonsense', and nothing in the world is worth taking seriously.[73] William thinks along the lines of Kant's concept of autonomy, where rational beings give themselves the moral law, whereas William's conception of autonomy has no room for laws – it consists only of *auto* and not of *nomos*. William's self-dissolving radicalization of autonomy can only lead to boredom because it contains no bounds and nothing is more boring than the boundless. His self-absorption knows no limits, and he wallows in an excess of aimless self-reflection. He lives from moment to moment, as a super-consumer of time, but the present is never related to past and future in any meaningful way. Therefore, William is unable to establish any sort of coherent whole that could create a basis for a personal identity.

Nobody can be anything more than a mirror for William, so all the flatness he believes that he finds everywhere around him is actually a reflection of himself. His narcissism reaches gargantuan proportions. His real, little ego is sadly inadequate, which is why he has to project a huge imaginary ego in order to compensate. The Romantic violates the world to escape his own nothingness; he ignores the boundaries that should be *between* himself and other people as well as the boundary that should keep himself and others *within* a shared world. William must overcome everything that differs from himself if he is to fully realize his freedom, to become one with the absolute, but he is a tragic hero because his project is doomed to failure. The transgression can never satisfy the longing from which it springs but inevitably makes even stronger. How can an empty self fill itself when it cannot recognize anything that differs from itself? When everything is subjugated by an all-too-powerful subject, everything becomes identical, and dreadfully boring. 'I am the only law of nature', writes William, 'and this law rules over everything. I lose myself in an immense, infinite desert.'[74] As a twisted quasi-Fichtean super-ego, William believes he can 'posit' the entire world, but in doing so he simply posits his own emptiness as a defining characteristic of the entire world. Nothing any longer can provide him with any sort of satisfaction, and the world appears to be completely impoverished.[75] It becomes a matter of indifference whether something is this or that. At the end of the *William Lovell*, the protagonist realizes just how misguided he has been: 'For a long time, I have attempted to make the other, the distant, my own property, and in doing so I have lost myself.'[76] When he is finally killed, the event is fairly insignificant, for in one sense he has been dead for a long time.

Another of William's friends, Mortimer, chooses medioc-rity,[77] but this only works as a sort of passive resignation, a resignation to remain bored. Or could this be the 'heroic' thing to do – to accept the state of the world, to accept bore-dom? This is a question I will deal with in chapter Four.

Patrick Bateman, the main character in Bret Easton Ellis's *American Psycho*,[78] is William Lovell 200 years on. Admittedly, William's list of sins is fairly modest compared to Bateman's run of sadistic murders,[79] for William merely murders a cou-ple of people, carries out some predatory raids, abducts a woman, commits fraud . . . The extreme scenes of murder and torture in *American Psycho* were necessary because the crimes carried out by William are fairly anodyne by today's stan-dards. Even so, William and Patrick are spiritual brothers who share boredom and transgression as their main perspectives on the world. Whereas the word *Langeweile* can be found on virtually every page of *William Lovell*, the term 'bored' only appears about ten times in *American Psycho*. Bateman is sick with boredom and resorts to bestiality in the hope of being able to get beyond this boredom.

The relationship between an aesthetic lifestyle, boredom, transgression and evil is clearly formulated in Stendhal's *On Love*:

One sees the ageing Don Juan blame the state of things, never himself, for his own satiety. One sees him being tormented by the poison that consumes him, carry on in all directions and continually change the object of his desire. But no matter what charisma he has, it is ulti-mately a choice between two evils – between still and bustling boredom. This is the sole choice left to him. Finally, he realises the fatal truth and admits it to himself, after which the only pleasure he has left is imposing his will on others, of doing evil for the sake of evil.[80]

Don Juan cannot, according to his own logic, blame himself for the boredom into which he has plunged ever more deeply because he has not wished for this to happen.[81] Patrick Bateman, too, claims that he is guiltless.[82] The transgression is ultimately neither liberating nor self-realizing, and yet is seems to the Romantic to be the only alternative.

Romanticism leads to existentialism, and the Romantic William Lovell claims 'My existence is the only conviction which is necessary for me.'[83] Sartre could easily have written that in *Being and Nothingness*. Perhaps I can reformulate the thesis: Romanticism is already existentialism and existentialism is incorrigibly Romantic. Of course, all of this is intimately connected to historical and political developments. With the emergence of the bourgeoisie and the death of God, man no longer set outs to serve something or someone else, but seeks to fulfil himself and gain his own happiness. The adventurousness of the Romantic is an aesthetic reaction to the monotony of the bourgeois world. The human subject is to be the source of all meaning and value, but it is still tied to the limitations of the physical world. The Romantic self attempts to overcome this situation by appropriating the entire world, i.e., by transgressing or negating all outer limits and rejecting all corrective standards outside himself. The Romantic self becomes a solipsistic self, one that has no belief in anything outside itself – for there cannot be any meaning other than what it has produced itself.

While Tieck seems to condone the acts of William Lovell – not in the sense of defending his misdeeds, but rather because, like Hölderlin, he harbours a deep respect for Romantic striving – Bret Easton Ellis rejects every aspect of Patrick Bateman. William is not a traditional villain. He has an unquenchable thirst for freedom, for fully realizing himself. This calls for a transgression of limits that are both outer (e.g. laws and customs) and inner (e.g. shame and conscience). He is, perhaps, the first fictional hero who consistently follows a transgressive logic. More of them were to follow, with Patrick Bateman as the most extreme to date.

The first words in *American Psycho* are 'ABANDON ALL HOPE YE WHO ENTER HERE.' We recognize this as the injunction above the gate to the Inferno in Canto III of Dante's *Commedia*. The final words of the novel are 'THIS IS NOT AN EXIT'.[84] The story is framed by these two sentences; as Bateman correctly observes: 'My life is a living hell.' But nobody ever listens to him when he points this out. One of the novel's mottos – taken from the song *(Nothing But) Flowers* by Talking Heads – is 'And as things fell apart / Nobody paid much attention.' There is no wholeness of meaning in *American Psycho*; all the events are like isolated atoms. The novel has a completely flat and episodic structure, without any genuine progression and an end that just tails off. It consists of little other than the affluent Patrick Bateman's descriptions of fashion, TV shows, murder, torture, drinks, superficial dialogues, etc. It is universe with no genuine qualitative differences, a world of levelling. And levelling creates boredom. One of the few episodes that has the strongest emotional impact on Bateman in the course of the novel is when one of his acquaintances has a smarter visiting card than himself.[85] Everybody in Bateman's world is the same. They are all rich and trim, with fine physiques.[86] Since everything appears to be the same, any difference, no matter how insignificant it would appear to be for the reader, becomes crucial for Bateman; he is, for example, full to bursting-point at the difference between two brands of mineral water![87] The only thing that matters is the surface: 'I feel like shit but look great.'[88]

Bateman is repeatedly described by others as 'the boy next door',[89] but he himself claims to be 'a fucking evil psychopath',[90] although without anyone paying any attention. His lack of identity is emphasised throughout the novel by his being confused with other people. Not even the doorman in his building seems to recognize his existence: 'I am a ghost to this man, I'm thinking. I am something unreal, something not quite tangible.' [91] And later in the novel, during dinner with a woman he later tortures and murders: 'I mean, does anyone really *see* anyone? Does anyone really *see* anyone else? Did *you* ever see *me*? *See*?' [92] He has no sense of personal identity, and attempts to achieve an identity by means of fashion and transgressions. The exteriorization of his personality is also indicated by his talking about himself in one chapter in the third person.[93] He compensates for a minimal self by consistently attempting to transgress, to expand. Bateman tries to establish a sense of identity by making subtle distinctions between different designer brands, but this is such an abstract, impersonal meaning that it cannot serve a genuinely individuating function. He therefore attempts to create an experience of a self by means of transgressions.

A distinction between transgression and transcendence could be useful here. Transgression simply means exceeding or going beyond a limit. It can be moderate or radical, but it always takes place within the same plane. Hence we can say that a transgression is always horizontal or flat. Transcendence, on the other hand, implies more of a qualitative leap into something radically other. The closest Bateman ever comes to transcendence is when he has a quasi-religious experience at a U2 concert:

> Suddenly I get this tremendous surge of feeling, this rush of knowledge and my own heart beats faster because of this and it's not impossible to believe that an invisible chord attached to Bono has now encircled me and now the audience disappears and the music slows down, gets softer, and it's just Bono onstage – the stadium's deserted, the band fades away.[94]

It is worth noting that this near-transcendence comes about without Bateman actively attempting to promote it – it forces itself on him from the outside. He first dismisses Bono's outstretched hand, but he finds himself affected nevertheless. Bono represents grace – grace can perfectly well assume an apparently trivial form, as Flannery O'Connor so brilliantly describes it in novels and short stories – but Bateman fails to hold on to the *moment*. He does not gain redemption, like Faust for example, but falls back into world and feels that information about business transactions is more important than the bond with Bono. The *moment* does not last, for there is no room for the moment in Bateman's world, as his deep boredom stifles even mystical experiences, and he slides back into immanence. For Patrick, transgression not transcendence is what counts. The problem is that after a while transgression ceases to mean anything to him; the atrocious is no longer capable of creating any sort of feeling in him.[95]

Patrick is like all the others around him, except that he is more extreme, and he also seems to suffer more under the all-embracing shallowness. Let us take a closer look at a passage near the end of the novel, where Patrick formulates something which can be taken as his philosophical outlook on life:

where there was nature and earth, life and water, I saw a desert landscape that was unending, resembling some sort of crater, so devoid of reason and light and spirit that the mind could not grasp it on any sort of conscious level and if you came close the mind would reel backward, unable to take it in. It was a vision so clear and real and vital to me that in its purity it was almost abstract. This was what I could understand, this was how I lived my life, what I constructed my movement around, how I dealt with the tangible. This was the geography around which my reality revolved: it did not occur to me, *ever*, that people were good or that a man was capable of change or that the world could be a better place through one's taking pleasure in a feeling or a look or a gesture, of receiving another person's love or kindness. Nothing was affirmative, the term 'generosity of spirit' applied to nothing, was a cliché, was some kind of bad joke. Sex is mathematics. Individuality no longer an issue. What does intelligence signify? Define reason. Desire – meaningless. Intellect is not a cure. Justice is dead. Fear, recrimination, innocence, sympathy, guilt, waste, failure, grief, were things, emotions, that no one felt anymore. Reflection is useless, the world is senseless. Evil is its only permanence. God is not alive. Love cannot be trusted. Surface, surface, surface was all that anyone found meaning in . . . this was civilisation as I saw it, colossal and jagged . . .[96]

God is dead, the world is devoid of meaning, justice is dead and sexuality fully quantified, reduced to a question of how much and how many. This is Bateman's world. There is nothing but surface, and this surface has no depth at all. How could one possibly find meaning in such a world? His answer is to push it to its limits and beyond, to transgress every conceivable and inconceivable limit, in order to create differences and thereby transgress the levelling. By wading in gore and ripping out guts, Bateman feels he actually manages to get hold of something *real*. 'This is my reality. Everything outside of this is like some movie I once saw.'[97] Reality slips away from him, and the reader is unable to determine with any certainty what Bateman really does and what he merely imagines, for there is no corrective standard outside his own, solipsistic reality: 'This is simply how the world, *my* world, moves.'[98] Such a solipsism is fully in compliance with traditional existentialist thought, with the use of such terms as 'anxiety', 'dread', 'nausea', etc. Anxiety especially plays a central role in *American Psycho*. Bateman mentions a 'nameless dread' on a number of occasions.[99] He says 'something about various forms of dread' to his secretary, without specifying further.[100] This dread has little metaphysical depth. On one occasion he has an attack of anxiety because there are too many films to choose from in a video shop. The banality of the anxiety, however, does not make it any the less serious for the person affected by it. Bateman's evil probably has its roots in this feeling of *dread*. In C. Fred Alford's insightful study, *What Evil Means to Us*, precisely the feeling of dread is emphasised as a common feature of evil.[101]

The world appears to be completely contingent for Bateman, and all his acts seem to be completely random. He repeatedly claims that there is no ultimate reason for doing one thing rather than another. Everything he has previously learnt – 'principles, distinctions, choices, morals, compromises, knowledge, unity, prayer – all of it was wrong, without any final purpose.'[102] The politically correct pronouncements that Patrick reels off have no substance and no relation at all to the life he is actually living. As when he says that it is vital to promote a return to traditional values and social conscience, and to fight materialism.[103]

There are three chapters in the book on music, for music is one of Bateman's main interests: one on Genesis, one on Whitney Houston and one on Huey Lewis and the News. In other words, he has a terrible taste in music. These chapters are interesting because the appalling banalities Bateman reels off about this music are actually more profound and mature than he normally is himself. He is deeply moved by a song by Genesis that expresses 'loneliness, paranoia and alienation', but also a 'hopeful humanism'.[104] Lacking an emotional life of his own, the banal music becomes a surrogate. For instance, he praises Huey Lewis and the News for singing so much about love instead of posing as young nihilists.[105] He is deeply moved by Whitney Houston's *The Greatest Love of All*, which he claims approaches the sublime and expresses a crucial message to mankind: 'Its universal message crosses all boundaries and instils one with the hope that it's not too late for us to better ourselves, to act kinder. Since it is impossible in the world to empathize with others, we can always empathize with ourselves. It's an important message, crucial really.'[106] This nonsense naturally has an ironic effect in the novel. Where Bateman attempts to show some real depth, his abnormal shallowness is revealed.

It is also worth noting a song by Madonna, *Like a Prayer*, which Bateman hears several times: 'life is a mystery, everyone must stand alone.'[107] Bateman is alone in the world, cut off from any human contact that goes beyond the uncompromisingly superficial, and his life is incomprehensibly flat. Bateman's existential exile and lack of a real world, make any empathic relation to other people impossible, but they also drain him of all humanity:

> I had all the characteristics of a human being – flesh, blood, skin, hair – but my depersonalization was so intense, had gone so deep, that the normal ability to feel compassion had been eradicated, the victim of a slow, purposeful erasure. I was simply imitating reality, a rough resemblance of a human being, with only a dim corner of my mind functioning.[108]

He writes about his own 'virtual absence of humanity'.[109] Bateman has in fact a certain degree of self-knowledge, and realizes that he has no substance, but argues that it has been impossible to reach any sort of deeper understanding of himself.[110] The impossibility stems from the fact that there is no depth there to understand, other than a desperate sense of boredom. No rational analysis can tell him who he is, for 'there . . . is . . . no . . . key'.[111]

Hegel makes the point that as soon as a certain level of self-consciousness is reached, a need for an identity emerges. Such an identity can exist in many different variants; the important thing for the present concern is that the lack of such an identity is incompatible with leading a meaningful life. Bateman's perversities make up his absolutely hopeless attempt at overcoming boredom in a world that contains no personal meaning for him.

I have already commented on the lack of any real narrative structure in *American Psycho*, that it consists of a series of isolated events. This reflects Bateman's fragmented sense of self, that he is incapable of telling his story with anything like a substantial narrative thread. Personal identity presupposes narrative identity, i.e., that one is capable of telling a relatively coherent story about oneself.[112] This is precisely what Bateman lacks. He has no personal history, and, as far as he knows, does not participate in any suprapersonal history, either. The lack of a real history with a past and a future necessitates Bateman's search for identity in whatever is around him at any given moment. Coherent experience presupposes a narrative dimension, but Bateman lacks the ability to narrate, and he is therefore incapable of transforming the incidents that surround him into a coherent *narrative*. He is unable to provide the reader with anything more than a wealth of *information*.

As absolutely individual, without God or a soul, only brand-names appear to be able to individuate Bateman. He is totally individuated, so monadic that his taste is utterly impersonal. A strange dialectic interaction occurs between abstraction and individuation. We are much too individual and lose a cultural overall meaning – what we could call an inter-meaning.[113] The only available meaning is to be found at a completely abstract level, and is represented by brands such as Dolce & Gabbana, Prada, Armani, Ralph Lauren, Hugo Boss, Versace, DKNY and Paul Smith. As Georg Simmel points out, dependence on fashion indicates the insignificance of the own personality, that a person is incapable of individuating himself.[114]

Such a process of abstract individuation cannot establish significant meaning in life. In order to live a meaningful life, humans need answers, i.e., a certain understanding of basic existential questions. These 'answers' do not have to be made completely explicit, as a lack of words does not necessarily indicate a lack of understanding, but one has to able to place oneself in the world and build a relatively stable identity. The founding of such an identity is only possible if one can tell a relatively coherent story about who one has been and who one intends to be. Time – as a unity of past, present and future – creates a unity in the self, and time and self are connected by means of a narrative. To have a personal identity is to have some representation of a narrative thread in life, where past and future can provide the present with meaning. I do not believe that meaning and identity can be properly understood independently of time and narrativity. To have an identity, to be a self, requires that one is capable of telling a story about oneself, about who one has been, who one wants to become and who one is now between past and future. To narrate is an ethical practice. As this kind of narrator, one is a *parrhesiast*, a truth-teller. One is primarily telling oneself the truth about oneself. However, in order to be able to tell such a story, one must also be able to relate to others.

We are all spiritually related to Lovell and Bateman, but we possess certain abilities that they lack – the ability to create purely symbolic expressions for our discontentment in civilization and the ability to recognize essential limits outside ourselves. It is these abilities that can keep the Romantic at arm's length from barbarism. I do not think we can come up with fully convincing fundamental reasons for maintaining such boundaries, but we can provide a pragmatic justification: the alternative is worse.

In many ways, Patrick Bateman is a classical existentialist hero, as is William Lovell. Existentialism typically claims that only individual life has value and can create values, but precisely because these values are left entirely to the individual to determine, they are completely arbitrary. From an existentialist point of view, an existence that does not primarily confirm its self and its own existence would be virtually valueless. However, as we have seen in the case of both Lovell and Bateman, such a referring back of all values to the sphere of one's own personality in effect drains everything of value and substance. So we would appear to be in an impossible situation, where we neither can seek the meaning we need within ourselves nor in anything outside ourselves – in fashion, for example. Without such a meaning, we search for every conceivable kind of meaning-substitute outside ourselves, but we are well aware that they never last. To get rid of this lack of duration we are always on the lookout for something new, so as to keep things going as long as possible.

This condition of meaning-crisis confronts most of us. We seek all sorts of meaning-substitutes, always embracing something new so as to create the illusion of meaning. We seek our identity in ephemeral objects, thereby equating identity with the transitory. The modern process of liberation ends up by obliterating the very identity it was supposed to liberate. We lead our lives as full-time tourists. As Zygmunt Bauman describes the modern subject: 'A tourist always, on holiday and in daily routine. A tourist everywhere, abroad and at home. A tourist in society, a tourist in life – free to do his or her own aesthetic spacing and forgiven the forgetting of the moral one. Life as the tourist's haunt.'[115] The process of liberation and the meaning-crisis is intertwined.

A central motif in modernity is the liberation from tradition. Traditions have been replaced by lifestyles. The concept of a lifestyle sounds trivial, but it is crucial for understanding modern life.[116] A lifestyle is essentially a set of practices maintained for a period of time. Modern man must choose a lifestyle, but, as it is based on a choice, one can simply choose to replace one lifestyle by another. This marks an essential difference in comparison with a tradition. A tradition is *inherited*, it is not something one chooses or rejects.[117] Traditions brings continuity to one's existence, but this sort of continuity is precisely what has been increasingly lost throughout modernity. The current norm is an unrestricted pluralism. We are free to choose as we like without having to make any lasting commitment to the chosen. And as a *style*, it is clear that the choice of a lifestyle is fundamentally a question of aesthetics. 'The world is the tourist's oyster. The world is there to be lived pleasurably – and thus be given meaning. In most cases, the aesthetic meaning is the only meaning it needs – and can bear' (Bauman again).[118] But this very process – of making all qualities *aesthetic*, of making all identities free from the chains of tradition – drains the world of meaning as its occupies the entire world, leaving less and less room for non-aesthetic qualities. Baudrillard claims that 'all the world's insignificance has been transfigured by the aestheticizing process.'[119] But, as he is well aware, an insignificance remains insignificant even though it has been aestheticized.

I cannot disagree with what Bauman says here – in terms of diagnosis, that is. My only quibble is his identification of this state with postmodernism, since I would say that originally it is not so much postmodern as Romantic. Even though postmodernism as an ideology is a thing of the past and has been for some time, Romanticism persists. What Bauman describes as postmodern is a Romanticism that had reached its full, self-annihilating potential. Where the Enlightenment focused on the similarities between all humans – for example, with regard to reason, as in Kant – Romantic thought emphasised the dissimilarities between individuals. This was to some extent already a postmodern approach: to focus on individuality rather than universality and on heterogeneity rather than homogeneity.

Romanticism contains an anti-Romantic element, however: an insight into its own basic failings. An example of this is William Lovell's failure to reach redemption. It is also made explicit in certain texts, such as in Novalis's strange little treatise, *Die Christenheit oder Europa*, which was written in the autumn of 1799 and published posthumously.[120] Polemically, Novalis argues that the Middle Ages was a time of greatness, because Christianity then united all men under one common interest. The problem was, however, that humanity was still unready for such a community and it dissolved into countless special interests. One of Novalis's best-known quotations is from his novel *Heinrich von Ofterdingen*: 'Where are we going? Always home.' (*Wo gehn wir denn hin? Immer nach Hause.*) But, as Thomas Wolfe said, 'You can't go home again.' Novalis was not so naive as to believe that one could simply return to the unified culture of the Middle Ages, but he believed that the old and the new Europe could be transformed into a new, third Europe, where a common Christian faith would unite all Europeans. Of course, Novalis was exaggeratedly optimistic in his forecast here, too, but more important for our subject was that even he, perhaps the most extreme of all the Jena Romantics, came to realize that Romantic individualism and fragmentation were ultimately untenable.

God, however, could not be brought back to life again. Towards the end of his Jena work *Glauben und Wissen*, Hegel – admittedly in a slightly different context than the one I am interested in here – wrote that 'recent religion depends on the feeling: God himself is dead.'[121] This death announcement was of course made much more ostentatiously by Nietzsche 80 years later,[122] but it was the point of departure for Jena Romanticism. The death of God does not place humanity in a world that is unambiguously given, but rather in a world where these very *limits* become privileged objects of experience, limits that can be posited, transformed and transgressed.[123] This, then, is the specifically modern experience – that of limits and transgressions.

ON BOREDOM, BODY, TECHNOLOGY AND
TRANSGRESSION: *CRASH*

David Cronenberg's 1996 film *Crash* is based on J. G. Ballard's 1973 novel of the same name. The novel, where the male main character is named after the author himself, gave rise to controversies. The reaction of one reader in Ballard's publishing house was symptomatic: 'This author is beyond psychiatric help. Do Not Publish!'

In the preface to *Crash*, Ballard writes that the relation between fiction and reality is in the process of being reversed, that we to an increasing extent living in a world of fictions (especially due to the influence of TV and commercials) and that the task of the author is therefore not to invent a fiction, for fictions are already there, but rather to invent reality.[124]

Why do we need reality? It is difficult to find an answer to that question, but it is a fact that we have such a need. *Crash* takes up the relation between reality, boredom, technology and transgressions. One of the main characters in *Crash*, Vaughan, claims that all prophecies are 'ragged and dirty'. The same can be said about *Crash*. A characteristic feature of most of Ballard's works is that he singles out aspects in the world of today, projects them into a future where they have developed further, and then returns them to the present: 'The future is a better key to the present than the past.'[125] Ballard is first and foremost someone who makes a diagnosis and, like most such persons, he is a moralist. As he put it in an article of 1969, we use our moral freedom to pursue our psychopathologies as a game. He even goes so far as to claim that what our children most have to fear is not death on the highway but rather our desire to calculate the most elegant parameters for their death.[126] In another article from the same year he wrote 'Certainly, Nazi society seems strangely prophetic of our own – the same maximizing of violence and sensation, the same alphabets of unreason and the fictionalizing of experience.'[127] Such statements must be kept in mind when seeking to interpret *Crash*.

In an interview in 1995 Ballard remarked:

People believe in nothing. There is nothing to believe in now . . . There's this vacuum . . . what people have most longed for, which is the consumer society, has come to pass. Like all dreams that come to pass, there is a nagging sense of emptiness. So they look for anything, they believe in any extreme. Any extremist nonsense is better than nothing . . . Well, I think we're on the track to all kinds of craziness. I think there is no end to what sort of nonsense will come out of the woodwork, and a lot of very dangerous nonsense. I could sum up the future in one word, and that word is boring. The future is going to be boring.[128]

In a world of emptiness, extremism will stand out as an attractive alternative to boredom. An underlying premise in the world of today would seem to be: Extreme conditions call for extreme measures. Ballard comes close to Nietzsche's assertion that man rather wants to create a grand Nothing than not to want at all, for one needs to have a goal.[129]

As I pointed out in chapter One, there is ample evidence for boredom as a cause of violence. Destruction equals life whereas boredom equals death. Arthur Miller describes how the 'misfit' turned to violence as an escape from boredom, how he 'stuck with his boredom, stuck inside it, until for two or three minutes he "lives"; he goes on raid around the corner and feels the thrill of risking his skin or his life as he smashes a bottle filled with gasoline on some kid's head. It is life . . . standing around with nothing coming up is as close to dying as you can get.'[130] Transgressions present themselves as the only cure for boredom.

Crash is a boring novel about people who are bored. A world that has become totally objectivized and stripped of all qualities cannot be anything else than boring. To transgress this boredom, man goes in for ever more extreme transgressions, thus following the Romantic mode of existence I outlined earlier.

The film version had its world premiere at Cannes in 1996, where it won the Special Jury Prize 'For Originality, For Daring, and For Audacity'. In the debate about *Crash* one got the impression that the film was mainly about a speculative presentation of sex and violence on the screen. Admittedly, it does not comprise much else, but in terms of the content, the film is rather quiet and contemplative. There are no typical film-effects, such as exploding cars or crash scenes in slow motion etc. *Crash* is extremely disturbing, however, and can hardly be accused of pandering to the public. Its point of departure lacks precisely the characteristics that would guarantee a commercial success. You encounter a cool, metallic quality as early as the credit titles, where there are large, cold silver letters against a silver-blue background, and Howard Shore's metallic film music fits the cold images perfectly as they are reduced to a minimum and do not feature a single pop song. For anyone prepared to let the film do its work, it opens up a space for self-reflection in terms of values that we cannot accept and are almost forced to reject. At the same time, most of us have to admit to being fascinated by what is being portrayed on the screen. The characters react in ways that are undeniably alien and despicable, but not *completely* alien, to most of us. The psychopathologies in *Crash* are in a certain sense our own, but they are taken to an extreme. The characters in the film deliberately provoke car crashes in order to get closer to reality, themselves and others. One of the main reasons why *Crash* upsets the viewer, is that it lacks the explicit sentimentality that characterizes most films. Maiming and death are followed by sexual excitement rather than the sorrow one would expect. The scenes involving sexual intercourse are cold and technical, rather like pistons going in and out. Sexuality is almost exclusively referred to in clinical terms. All the characters are lost in existence; they use sexuality as an area where they believe, or at least hope, they will be able to find themselves again. There is something correct about Cronenberg's observation here, since we – especially because of psychoanalysis – have been indoctrinated into believing that sexuality is the key to who we are, that it contains the deepest secrets about ourselves. Cronenberg is disturbed about modern sexuality. Any viewer capable of looking beyond the twisted metal and the mixture of semen, blood and motor-oil can see that *Crash* is a moralistic critique of modern civilization. The moral dimension is communicated indirectly. In the universe of the film itself there is no possibility of adopting an ethical attitude in the Kierkegaardian sense, only one that is predominantly aesthetic, and possibly religious.

The film does not have any distinct plot. The completely 'linear' action begins with Catherine Ballard taking out one of her breasts and laying it on the cool metal wing of an aircraft in a hangar; her male partner then penetrates her from behind without their exchanging a single glance. In the next scene James Ballard penetrates his camera girl from behind and their eyes never meet. In the next scene James penetrates Catherine from behind – while they both look down on all the cars on the motorway and tell each other about their erotic escapades. Catherine asks James if the camera girl got an orgasm, and James tells her that she did not. Catherine says: 'Maybe the next one.' This sentence is repeated by James in the final scene of the film, and is of great significance. It is worth noting the absence of shared eye-contact – it is as if the characters are completely detached from each other. James and Catherine Ballard's marriage is reduced to sex alone, and not even that is particularly satisfying. They are suffering from *taedium sexualitatis*, and their promiscuity leaves them profoundly bored. As James puts it in the novel: 'I thought of my last forced orgasms with Catherine, the sluggish semen urged into her vagina by my bored pelvis.'[131] He also describes their sex life as 'almost totally abstracted', maintained only by fantasies and perversities.

While out driving James loses control of his car, ends up in the opposite lane and is involved in a head-on collision with Dr Helen Remington and her husband. When James wakes up in hospital, he describes the accident as a 'relief', as after an orgasm. At the bedside Catherine jerks off James while describing the look and smell of the car. James recovers, and meets Helen once more. He buys himself a new car, the same model as the former one, and he and Helen have sex in it, as if attempting to repeat the sexual intensity of their first collision. Through the experience of the crash, they have both become aware of new erotic opportunities opened up by the relationship between sex and risk. They have both been significantly changed by the crash, and Helen is now incapable of having an orgasm anywhere but in a car.

Helen brings James in touch with Vaughan, the high-priest of a small cult devoted to the combination of sex and car crashes. Vaughan methodically maps all possible varieties of crashes, in order to perform them. He also wishes to drive cars that have been involved in famous accidents, such as Albert Camus' Facel Vega, or Grace Kelly's Rover 3500. To begin with, he has to make do with driving a large 1963 Lincoln convertible – the same type as the one in which Kennedy was assassinated. Admittedly, Kennedy's death cannot really be called an accident, but his death is, nevertheless, a car-related one with a distinct aura. Vaughan wants to transfer the aura of previous accidents to his own life, which seems to have no content at all.

We meet Vaughan when, with his assistant, he is to repeat James Dean's death crash, which took place in California on 30 September 1955. He has procured an exact replica of Dean's car *Little Bastard*, a Porsche 550. Vaughan and Seagrave are also planning to copy the crash that killed Jayne Mansfield in 1967. Vaughan initially claims that his project consists of an exploration of 'the reshaping of the human body by modern technology', but he later dismisses this description as superficial and says 'A car crash is a fertilizing rather than a destructive event.' It is a fertilizing event because it ostensibly comprises a huge emission of sexual energy. The question is, however, whether these two descriptions of the project are all that far from each other. The crash is necessary because 'ordinary' sexual practices have become insufficient and boring. The human body is no longer capable of satisfying itself and must seek assistance from technology to reach a climax. There is a common misunderstanding that technology is external to ourselves, that man and technology can be separated. But man, the technical object and the outside world form a continuum. We spontaneously relate to ourselves and the world by means of the technical object.

The problem is that a shift has occurred in this continuum between man, the technical object and the outside world, placing too much emphasis on the middle state, hence reducing the polarity between man and world. Such a lack of polarity is also characteristic of boredom. There can be an otherness only insofar as there can be an ownness and vice versa. If the polarity between the two is lost, everything becomes identical, indifferent and immanent. Technology and boredom are related, and seem to gain strength from each other. Technology dominates a large part of our relationship to the world.

Man wears prostheses. In the twentieth century, the car in particular has stood out as being such a prosthesis, as an extension of a limited body. There are today about 500 million private cars moving about on the face of the earth. This represents a strange relationship between technology, prostheses and death. James tellingly describes a car as 'my own metal body',[132] thereby echoing Ernst Jünger's claim that 'Technology is our uniform.'[133] A prosthesis always points to man's mortality. Not because it is technical – for the categories of technology never allow any understanding of death – but by virtue of the interface between the prosthesis and the body. The prosthesis demonstrates man's basic finitude. That is why we attempt to hide those prostheses that most directly replace bodily functions, such as artificial legs and hearing aids. In *Crash*, on the other hand, the prostheses are worn with maximum visibility, clearly in order to illustrate one's mortality.

Anthropocentrism gave rise to boredom, and when anthropomorphism was replaced by technocentrism, boredom became even more profound. Technology involves the dematerialization of the world, where things disappear into pure functionality. We have long since passed a stage where we could keep track of technology. We scurry along behind, as is perhaps particularly clear in IT, where hardware and software have always become obsolete before most of the users have learned how to use them. *Crash* describes a universe where technology has taken over the world as a whole. There is no profundity in *Crash*, nor any doubling of reality. Everything is exactly what it is and nothing else. Although I ought directly to add that it is very misleading to claim that everything is what it is and nothing else, for this would seem to imply that things have an identity, when it is precisely this that they lack. Things no longer have any being. Everything is something else than itself, i.e., things gain their identity via something else, namely their symbolic value. As I mentioned earlier, the *qualitas* of things is to be found on the great rubbish tip of history. In a culture determined by pure functionality and efficiency, boredom will rule because the quality of the world disappears in the pantransparency, in the all-embracing diaphanousness. In such a culture, experiments with sex and drugs – or escapes into the fog of new religion, for that matter – will appear tempting, because they seem to offer a way out of a piteously boring everyday life and a way into something that goes beyond the banal. The sad thing is that these excesses can never satisfy the longing out of which they spring.

In *Crash*, sexuality fulfils itself in death. The characters do not flee from their own mortality but embrace it wholeheartedly, as if only death can give their lives a hint of meaning. It is through death, through the ultimate destruction of one's self, that the self is finally individuated. According to a traditional, Cartesian dualism, the identity of the body will be only of minor importance, because identity here has primarily to do with the soul, not the body. But if the body is what one is supposed to be identical with, the question of the identity of the body becomes precarious. For we have abandoned searching within ourselves, and have now begun searching in the external world – a characteristic of 'modern, average nihilism', according to Karl Jaspers.[134] In the world of the film, the self can only be grounded in the body, but at the same time the body is insufficient on its own and has to be supplemented, mediated by technology. But this technology also leads to death, and this movement towards the self is paradoxical because it is also a movement towards final self-annihilation. As Karl Kraus so aptly puts it: 'The true wonder of technology is that it honestly destroys that for which it compensates.'[135]

In the last scene of *Crash*, James uses Vaughan's wrecked car to force Catherine off the road. He runs down to her car and crawls under it in order to lie there beside her. She is alive. 'Maybe the next one, darling . . . Maybe the next one', says James. These are the final words spoken in the film. What will maybe happen the next time? In the light of the first scene with James and Catherine, it would seem reasonable to interpret it as an orgasm. The relationship between eroticism and death has been made explicit by Georges Bataille:

> If the union of two lovers comes about through love, it involves the idea of death, murder or suicide. This aura of death is what denotes passion. On a lower level than this implied violence – a violence matched by the separate individual's sense of continuous violation – the world habit and shared egotism begins, another mode of discontinuity, in fact. Only in the violation, through the death if need be, of the individual's solitariness can there appear that image of the beloved in which the lover's eyes invests all being with significance.[136]

Death can be that of the one or the other. The intertwining of death and desire finds eccentric expression in *Penthesileia* by Heinrich von Kleist, where Penthesileia simply confuses the two in her deranged state of mind and slits Achilles' throat. She then says:

> It was then a confusion. Kiss and bite
> Resemble one another, and the one
> Who deeply loves can well confuse the two.

Kierkegaard noted in his diary that 'There are insects which die at the very moment of fertilization. Like this, all happiness, the highest moment of pleasure in life, is accompanied by death.'[137] Or as Foucault put it in one of his last interviews:

> I think that I have real difficulty in experiencing pleasure.

I think that pleasure is a very difficult form of behaviour. It is not as simple as that to enjoy oneself. And I must say that that is my dream. I would like and I hope I'll die of an overdose of pleasure of any kind. Because I think it's difficult and I always have the feeling that I do not feel *the* pleasure, the complete total pleasure and, for me, it's related to death.[138]

In *Crash* scars are trophies from accidents. In a world of polished, machine-like bodies, only scars can individuate the body (and the machine).[139] Destruction, whether it be of human bodies or machines, creates a rift in hyperreality and opens up an outside, a window to reality. James says: 'The crash was the only real experience I had been through for years.'[140] To destroy someone or something is a way of confirming its existence.[141]

In the crash, the order of traffic breaks down, and reality reveals itself in the form of naked materiality. It is almost as if the breakdown in technology brings reality closer. T. S. Eliot wrote that 'human kind cannot bear very much reality',[142] and this is right in a way. But the opposite is also true: human kind cannot bear too *little* reality. All the bodies in *Crash* are strangers to themselves, and only by means of scars and wounds can the body be regained as one's own body.

The characters in *Crash* are not emotionally dead – if they were, they would have no interest in crashes. It is more that they are unable to get in touch with themselves or others in any other way than by aestheticizing pain. As a character puts in *The Atrocity Exhibition*: 'Sex is now only a conceptual act, it's probably only in terms of the perversions that we can make contact with each other at all.'[143] They have all lost themselves, and attempt to recover the relation to themselves and others by crashes and sexual excesses. This is especially clear in the final scene of the film version of *Crash*, which is not in the novel. When all is said and done,

Crash is an optimistic film because it implicitly claims that meaning can be restored. James and Catherine both believe that they can re-find each other, but they also believe that this is possible only if they re-invent each other in a certain sense – that they can find each other through new practices.

Crash is very much concerned with the concept of transgression. A transgression is a movement towards and beyond a point or a limit that reveals new limits that can or must be transgressed. The final limit that cannot be transgressed is God or the Absolute. In *Crash* death or orgasm has the status of the Absolute that cannot be transgressed. The interface is the body. There is no longer any search for the infinite, but rather for the finite, and death or orgasm become the immanently holy – and absolute transcendence is consigned to history.

One's own death can never be a clear *object* for consciousness, and that is precisely why only death can represent transcendence in a world where immanence has become total and an outside has been completely eradicated. In a world of immanence, nothing genuinely new can come into being, and the only option left is to hold on to, or attempt to increase, an already existing meaning. One way of doing this is by means of repetitions. Certain events are perceived as containing such a wealth of meaning that a repetition of them should be able to transfer this meaning to the repetitor. That is the reason why Vaughan stages death-crash classics.

Boredom is mainly defined by the present, or rather: boredom knows neither past nor future, whereas melancholy is characterized by a longing for a time that once existed (or possibly a future that is hoped for). Using Kierkegaard's terminology, we can see that the melancholic is someone who lives in the memory, i.e., someone who repeats backwards, while true repetition takes place forwards.[144] Neither repetition backwards nor forwards is applicable to boredom, whose very nature is recurrence and not true repetition. Boredom is pure immanence, whereas genuine repetition is transcendence.[145] This transcendence leads to happiness, Kierkegaard claims.[146] And he even says, acutely, that if the repetition is not possible, human life dissolves into empty, meaningless noise.[147] In *Crash* an attempt is made to use repetition to transcend boredom. The question is whether this is feasible. James's actions should perhaps be understood as a teleological suspension of the ethical, to continue Kierkegaard's terminology, i.e., that ethics is put to one side in order to attain to a higher goal. If so, James's actions will be a kind of perverse extension of Abraham's willingness to sacrifice Isaac. Should James's attempt to force Catherine off the road then be regarded as based on a sincere *belief* that the crash will not kill her, but rather re-establish their intimacy?

Whereas Ballard's novel seems to conclude that genuine repetition is impossible, Cronenberg's film version is optimistic because it seems to conclude that genuine repetition is possible, that James and Catherine *can* re-establish their original relationship. The film suggests that the immediate, represented by the intimacy between James and Catherine, can be repeated.[148] If repetition alone is capable of transcending immanence and repetition is held to be possible, the film also claims that transcendence is possible. But does not this transcendence comes across as being tacked on? Should *Crash* not have ended with the same words as *American Psycho*: 'This is not an exit', rather than 'Maybe the next one'?

Boredom always contains an awareness of being trapped, either in a particular situation or in the world as a whole. Any attempt to make a radical break with boredom seems to be in vain because all such attempts will be events within a totality of boredom. A mood cannot be modified by means of an exercise of will, but only by being replaced by another mood. Moods, however, cannot simply be chosen as we see fit. This is clearly seen in *Crash* the novel, but is perhaps less obvious in *Crash* the film, which is far more optimistic. Does this transcendence not just remain as an assertion, or a purely logical possibility? Is it not clear that all the characters in *Crash* are driving at full speed into a cul de sac, and that they rather ought to sit down and wait for a moment that will probably never come?

SAMUEL BECKETT AND THE
IMPOSSIBILITY OF PERSONAL MEANING

In Karl Rosenkranz's much discussed, though seldom read, *Ästhetik des Häßlichen* from 1853, we find something that seems undeniably to prefigure the work of Samuel Beckett. Rosenkranz talks about boredom as being ugly – something that is common enough – but, surprisingly, he goes on to claim that in the boring there lies an opening to the comic:

> The boring is ugly, or rather: Ugliness to the point of the dead, empty, tautological awakens a feeling of boredom in us. The beautiful allows us to forget time, because, as something eternal and self-sufficient, it also transports us to eternity and thus fills us with bliss. But if the emptiness of a view becomes so great that we begin to pay attention to time as time, we notice the lack of content of pure time – and this feeling is boredom. Boredom is not comic in itself, but a turn-around towards the comic occurs when the tautological and boring are produced as self-parody and irony.[149]

Is it not precisely this that is investigated so brilliantly by Beckett? The word 'boredom' is not used very often in his literary works.[150] We do, however, find a discussion of boredom in Beckett's *Proust*, which is strongly influenced by Schopenhauer. There Beckett considers the fundamental condition of life as a pendulum movement between suffering and boredom.[151] Large chunks of Beckett's work can indeed

be described as a comedy of boredom. This is perhaps especially obvious in *Waiting for Godot*. (I will spend less time on
the comedy of boredom in Beckett than on the prerequisite of
total boredom – the impossibility of personal meaning.)

Beckett wrote his essay on Proust when in his early twen-
ties. In it he has the following to say:

> Friendship is a social expedient, like upholstery or the dis-
> tribution of garbage buckets. It has no spiritual signifi-
> cance. For the artist, who does not deal in surfaces, the
> rejection of friendship is not only reasonable, but a neces-
> sity. Because the only possible spiritual development is in
> the sense of depth. The artistic tendency is not expansive,
> but a contraction. And art is the apotheosis of solitude.
> There is no communication because there are no vehicles
> of communication. Even on the rare occasions when word
> and gesture happen to be valid expressions of personality,
> they lose their significance on their passage through the
> cataract of the personality that is opposed to them. Either
> we speak and act for ourselves – in which case speech and
> action are distorted and emptied of their meaning by an
> intelligence that is not ours, or else we speak and act for
> others – in which case we speak and act a lie.[152]

Beckett chose the distortion, i.e., art. The antithesis he puts
forward here between honest isolation and dishonest sociality, and the inevitable lack of communication that results
from both, can be seen as definitive for all of his writings. As
he also says: 'We are alone. We cannot know and we cannot
be known.'[153] Every extrovertly uniting gesture is in vain. But
– and it is a 'but' in this case – we also have to continue, in
a vain hope of transgressing the own I, which increasingly
disintegrates.

This voice that speaks, knowing that it lies, indifferent to

what it says, too old perhaps and too abased ever to suc-
ceed in saying the words that would be its last, knowing
itself useless and its uselessness in vain, not listening to
itself but to the silence that it breaks and whence perhaps
one day will come stealing the long clear sigh of advent
and farewell, is it one? . . . It issues from me, it fills me, it
clamours against my walls, it is not mine, I can't stop it, I
can't prevent it, from tearing me, racking me, assailing
me. It is not mine, I have none, I have no voice and must
speak, that is all I know, it's round that I must revolve, of
that I must speak, with this voice that is not mine . . .[154]

'I have to speak, whatever that means. Having nothing to say,
so words but the words of others.'[155] A basic premise in
Beckett's works is that uttering a word is to utter the words
of others. 'Words, words, my life has never been anything
else than words.'[156] We are created out of the words of others and do not have any other choice. But we cannot even
simply repeat the words of others, for each time we repeat
them they become distorted and constantly distance themselves from their starting-point. This is why the quotations
in Beckett's texts are so often mis-quotations. Language is
not even any good when it comes to citations.[157]

All meaning consists of ever more pale copies of former
meaning. The only thing that is certain is that 'words fail'.[158]
'All life long the same questions, the same answers.'[159] 'I love
the old questions. Ah, the old questions, the old answers
there's nothing like them!'[160] This is what Beckett's works
consist of: old questions and old answers – and hardly even
that. These are a well-known theme we are already familiar
with from Ecclesiastes, but, as it says in *Malone Dies*:
'thoughts resemble each other so strikingly when you get to
know them.'[161] So Beckett is not particularly innovative in
this regard. The innovative element would have to be that he
has no faith in any of the answers, except that things have

gone terribly wrong. As he states in *Proust*, 'the only Paradise that is not the dream of a madman, the Paradise that has been lost.'[162]

There is a relationship between Beckett himself and the mad artist that Hamm talks about in *Endgame*:

> I once knew a madman who thought the end of the world had come. He was a painter – and engraver. I had a great fondness for him. I used to go and see him, in the asylum. I'd take him by the hand and drag him to the window. Look! There! All that rising corn! And there! Look! The sails of the herring fleet! All that loveliness! He'd snatch away his hand and go back into his corner. Appalled. All he had seen was ashes.[163]

Beckett anticipates the end of the world, but this dystopia is not particularly original, either.

> Saying is inventing. Wrong, very rightly wrong. You invent nothing, you think you are inventing, you think you are escaping, and all you do is stammer out your lesson, the remnants of a pensum one day got by heart and long forgotten . . .[164]

'Only what's been said exists. Apart from what's been said, nothing exists.'[165] We live in words, through words, created by words, the words of others. The words are never our own. We never become ourselves until the words fall silent, and then we fall silent, too. 'Where do they come from, these words that stream out of my mouth, and what do they mean?'[166] 'I've got to talk. I shall never be silent. Never.'[167] Language is a habit we are unable to free ourselves from, even though there is 'Little is left to tell.'[168] 'I use the words you taught me. If they don't mean anything any more, teach me others. Or let me be silent.'[169] To the extent that language conveys meaning, it is the meaning of others that is expressed. 'What does it matter who's speaking, someone said what does it matter who's speaking.'[170] But who is speaking is crucial, for the crucial thing is that it is not *me* who is speaking when I speak. 'All these voices are theirs, voices that rattle like chains in my head.'[171]

I have already defined modern boredom via the concept of an absence of personal meaning. In Beckett, this absence is total. His 'theory of meaning' is essentially this: There is no personal meaning, and all other meaning only becomes paler and paler until it is a nothing. What else is there to do than to wait or hope for a new meaning? The problem is that the waiting for meaning, for *the moment*, is endless. A real understanding of human existence has to be based on a fundamental absence of meaning.

According to Adorno, Beckett's work 'is an extrapolation of negative *kairos*. The fulfilled moment reverses into perpetual repetition that converges with desolation.'[172] Beckett focuses on a moment that is basically an absence. The moment (*kairos*) never comes. All we can do is wait, but unlike the waiting that is described in, for example, St Paul – which is a waiting for Christ's second coming, *parousia* – it is a waiting without a purpose. It is a waiting that is not defined by anything that is to come, but by something that will never come. For the positive *kairos*, the moment as openness to *parousia*, is purely imaginary, can never be fulfilled. Nor, though, can it be banished from thought, and it changes from a waiting for a positive moment to a waiting *in* a negative moment that lasts for ever. A waiting without time passing. A waiting *sub specie aeternitatis*, from the point of view of eternity.

It is not time in the usual sense that one is waiting for but a situation that at some point will arise. This future orientation means that time is not simply a time that passes but a time that *lasts* towards that which one is waiting for. When one waits, one is aware of time, and one waits for the time of waiting to come to an end. Obviously, one can wait without being bored as well as be bored without waiting, but waiting and boredom are often connected with each other. When we wait, our waiting has a purpose. We wait for *something*. But in Beckett it is a purposeless waiting, for although this is not always obvious to the characters in the plays or other writings, it is obvious to the reader that they are not waiting for anything at all. It is a waiting for something that will never come.

Beckett seeks to capture this nothingness, or absence. This absence is the emptiness around which his works revolve. As it says in the poem in the Addenda to the novel *Watt*:

> who may tell the tale
> of the old man?
> weigh absence in a scale?
> mete want with a span?
> the sum assess
> of the world's woes?
> nothingness
> in words enclose?[173]

There is *no* positiveness in Beckett's work. His literary universe consists of a language that gives less and less meaning and a metaphysical absence that does not give any meaning, as well as isolated 'subjects' that cannot give themselves any meaning. He distances himself from the Romantic conception of the self, which can powerfully spread out to fill itself. Beckett is no ordinary existentialist. He seeks to make a definitive break with the Romantic-existentialist conception of the self, where the I is able to redeem itself. The only thing that exists is time, too much time, in a universe where nothing has happened. 'Can there be anywhere else than this endless here?' [174] To be set to wait for a moment that will never come, in a world of immanence, with no outside at all. This is boredom taken to its logical conclusion.

How can one possibly overcome such a situation? It would have to be by managing to get oneself to stop yearning for the moment, but that is an ambition that one would never be able to realize fully:

> Longing the so-said mind long lost to longing. The so-missaid. So far so-missaid. Dint of long longing lost to longing. Long vain longing. And longing still. Faintly longing still. Faintly vainly longing still. For fainter still. For faintest. Faintly vainly longing for the least of longing. Unlessenable least of longing. Unstillable vain least of longing.
> Longing that all go. Dim go. Void go. Longing go. Vain longing that vain longing go.[175]

ANDY WARHOL: RENOUNCING PERSONAL MEANING

There is possibly one sure cure for boredom – to leave Romanticism behind and renounce all personal meaning in life. In a sense, this was what Beckett did, but his work concerns itself mostly with the vacuum that is left. It is, however, possible that this vacuum can be filled by an impersonal meaning that is kept impersonal – and which is therefore conceived as meaningless by us Romantics – without making any attempt to make it any more than that. One of those who has come closest to such an abandonment of Romanticism is Warhol. His attempt failed, but even so is worth examining it. (I deal exclusively with Warhol's public *persona*, out of respect for the work, for Warhol insisted that everything worth knowing about him could be found in the surfaces of his paintings, films and own self.) It is not easy to reconstruct a consistent 'philosophy' on the basis of Warhol's work, since it contains many paradoxes. Even so, I shall try to present it as cohesively as possible.

What fascinates me most about Warhol is his uncompromising insistence on meaninglessness. The days I spent ploughing through his diaries, where the word 'boring' occurs frequently, were perhaps the most boring of my life so far – they contain no profundity whatsoever, and there is nothing important on a single one of the 800 densely packed pages. Warhol and his work are so flat they are completely transparent, just as pornography is. Baudrillard reckons that Warhol 'was the first person to bring us modern fetishism, transaesthetical fetishism – to a picture without quality, a presence without desire.'[176] Warhol's art returns to a pre-Romantic paradigm of art, where expressiveness is not a relevant category. Warhol's work deals with the inner abstraction of things, with everything appearing as a flat echo of itself and Warhol empowering their spiritual emptiness. Apart from many of the paintings from the 1960s, especially the series of 'disaster paintings', there followed a monochrome canvas of the same size that further seems to underline the emptiness in the paintings. Everything is dead in Warhol, although sometimes there is something beautiful as well – when he succeeds in portraying the shoddy with a cool purity.

Warhol is beyond every form of alienation, since alienation always contains an echo of something allegedly authentic. Such an echo has died away in his work. He talked about his own film *Kitchen* (1965) as 'illogical, without motivation or character and completely ridiculous. Very much like real life.'[177] Warhol's art has to do with style and fashions, nothing else. He said: 'You can't be more superficial than me and live.' Warhol is devoid of any soul, and he removed the soul from everything he depicted, as is particularly obvious in the pictures of celebrities he did, when the person depicted has stiffened and become a flat icon, stripped of any depth. In the 15 minutes, it is the actual fame, not its content, that is of importance. Warhol's ideal picture of a human is an empty, impersonal figure that gains fame and makes a lot of money. He managed to fulfil this ambition himself, becoming something as paradoxical as an anonymous superstar. He defined the crux of his philosophy as 'looking for nothingness'.[178]

> I wake up and call B.
> B is anybody who helps me kill time.
> B is anybody and I'm nobody. B and I.[179]

> I'm sure I'm going to look into the mirror and see nothing. People are always calling me a mirror and if a mirror looks into a mirror, what is there to see? . . . Some critic called me the Nothingness Himself and that didn't help my sense of existence any. Then I realized that existence itself is nothing and I felt better.[180]

> The thing is to think of nothing . . . nothing is exciting, nothing is sexy, nothing is not embarrassing.[181]

> Everything is nothing.[182]

Warhol's obsession with nothingness was perhaps most clearly expressed in his own non-personality. Individualism had not got any real foothold before the Enlightenment and Romanticism and is thus historically contingent, but there is something paradoxical involved in doing away with one's own individuality, as Warhol attempted to do. This paradox is brilliantly and anachronistically portrayed in the Monty Python film *Life of Brian*. Brian stands talking to a huge crowd of people who have chosen him to be their prophet. Brian, who doesn't want the job, shouts down to them: 'You are all individuals!' The crowd replies in unison: 'Yes, we are all individuals!' The only exception is a man who says: 'I'm not!' The point is that every explicit break with an individualistic ideology must of necessity be individualistic, which does not get one very far. Warhol's life and work, his 'machinic snobbery',[183] is that sort of individualistic 'I am not an individual!'.

Warhol was himself well aware of this paradox. As he said in 1963: 'I want everybody to think alike . . . I think everybody should be a machine . . . Everybody just goes on thinking the same thing, and every year it gets more and more alike. Those who talk about individuality are the ones who most object to deviation, and in a few years it may be the other way round.'[184] I believe Warhol was right in his prophecy here. Deviation has even become conformist. Everyone today has to be 'something special', without *standing out* in any way at all. Deviation is boring. When individualism is conformist, conformism also becomes individualistic. Warhol's problem was that no matter how much he tried to get beyond individualism, he remained, by the very act of going beyond, in that which was to be transgressed and thus thrown back on himself as an individual. Warhol demanded that his gravestone should not be inscribed, a demand that was not respected by his surviving relatives, but a blank stone would also have been a strongly individualistic move.

Warhol is an anti-Romantic, but precisely for that reason his project is extremely Romantic, because it is linked to Romanticism by being its negative image. His pictorial world is an attempt to return to a pre-Romantic world. but God is just as absent, and the problem that led to the emergence of Romanticism is just as real. God had a more powerful meaning-providing force than Coca-Cola and Elvis, and no matter how beautiful Marilyn Monroe was, she was hardly in the same league as the Christ's Mother. The difference between pre-Romanticism and post-Romanticism is a difference in what symbolic capital is available to the symbolist. Warhol also became a worse and worse artist for every year that passed after the mid-1960s, because the symbols had less and less of their former potency. All that then is left is emptiness and boredom.

Sometimes I like to be bored, and sometimes I don't – it depends on what kind of mood I'm in. Everyone knows how it is: some days one can sit and look out the window for hours and hours and some days one can't sit still for a moment. I've been quoted a lot as saying, 'I like boring things.' Well, I said it and I meant it. But that does not mean I'm not bored by them. Of course, what I think is boring can't be the same as what other people think is, since I could never stand to watch all the most popular action shows on TV, because they're essentially the same plots and the same shots and the same cuts over and over again. Apparently, most people love watching the same basic thing, as long as the details are different. But I'm just the opposite: If I'm going to sit and watch the same thing I saw the night before, I don't want it to be essentially the same – I want it to be exactly the same. Because the more you look at the same exact thing, the more meaning goes away, and the better and emptier you feel.[185]

For Warhol, boredom was his fate, and he tried to do the same thing as Fernando Pessoa's heteronym, Bernardo Soares, namely 'to experience ennui in such a way that it does not hurt.'[186] The abandonment of personal meaning, the abandonment of every ambition driven by the idea that such a meaning can be gained, the abandonment of any such meaning possibly existing – this abandonment did not enable Warhol to get beyond boredom. On the contrary, he lived out boredom. Anyone who has once been smitten with Romanticism can never abandon it entirely. One cannot retrieve a lost innocence. And what was the result? 'The bored languor, the wasted pallor . . . the glamour rooted in despair, the self-admiring carelessness, the perfected otherness . . .'[187]

By completely ignoring the emotions, including boredom, the emotions were to be made to cease, hopefully to be replaced by a profound peace of mind, something close to the *ataraxia* of antiquity: 'I think that once you see emotions from a certain angle, you can never think of them as real again. That's what more or less has happened to me', said Warhol.[188] But anyone who has *felt* cannot forget what it is like to feel. There will always remain a longing or a nostalgia for personal meaning, for something that actually means something. 'Sex is nostalgia for sex.'[189] Sexuality is nothing more than a longing for a time when it meant something, and the Warhol ambition became to reduce it further, so that it no longer contained anything that reminded one of anything that could be called authentic – it becomes completely mechanical.

The goal is to do away with nostalgia, to relinquish the dream of the meaningful. 'People's fantasies are what gives them problems. If you didn't have fantasies you wouldn't have problems because you'd just take whatever was there.'[190] By simply becoming a flat reflection of his surroundings, by relinquishing every Romantic dream of something more, by forgetting everything that is past, by becoming sheer contemporaneity, Warhol hoped to avoid the sorrows and disappointments of life. But a fleeting contemporaneity cannot be anything else than boring. Warhol believed that forgetting will eradicate boredom, because forgetting will make everything new: 'I have no memory. Every day is a new day because I don't remember the day before.'[191] 'I wasn't bored because I had forgotten it already.'[192] Warhol believed that it is duration as such that makes life boring, and that the lasting can only be transgressed via the new.[193] But the new itself becomes routine and thus becomes boring. Adorno rightly pointed out that the category of the new is an abstract negation of the lasting and therefore coincides with it: the weakness shared by both is the invariant nature of them both.[194]

Warhol had one recipe that can always be used when life is on the point of breaking down. One simply says: 'So what?' One of the clearest expressions of this is perhaps the clinical suicide pictures where the fall into death is registered without a hint of morbid fascination or sadness. It is simply one vast 'So what?'[195] Warhol liked Kennedy because he was 'spirited, young, smart', but the only thing that worried him about the assassination was that everyone was 'programmed' to feel sad about it.[196] Sometimes Warhol gives the impression of possessing a stoic quality, but that would be mistaking stoicism with cynicism. Warhol was first and foremost a *voyeur*, a voyeur who surrounded himself with drugs, promiscuity and despair at The Factory, and who just looked on – and felt profoundly bored while doing so.[197] To the extent that transgression existed in Warhol himself, it was a voyeuristic transgression.

Warhol is perhaps also the person who takes furthest the manifesto of decadence from Baudelaire, Huysmans and Wilde. He gained maximum benefit out of displaying his own boredom, wearing it like an expensive piece of jewellery. He is reminiscent of Paul Valéry's Monsieur Teste, who, devoid of content, is almost pure non-existence.[198] Teste suffers from neither melancholy nor depression, but from a profound boredom. In boredom both the world and the personality are annihilated – something that is unusually evident in Teste. Teste, with his uncompromising conformity, is a better Warhol than Warhol himself, for Teste manages to give up every distinction between the inner and the outer, and to devote himself entirely to pure functionalism in relation to the world that surrounds him. Teste is a nothing. It seems as if Teste has *chosen* this boredom. Why? Perhaps to protect himself against the world by losing it. But anyone who has ever tasted the world cannot live in ignorance in its absence.

We can't go beyond the Romantic conception of ourselves *and* the world as one, as Warhol attempted to do. But we can modify it and try to reach a sort of clarification concerning the boredom that will inevitably afflict us. The last part of this book is devoted to that issue.

THREE

The Phenomenology of Boredom

By far the most elaborate phenomenological analysis of boredom is to be found in the series of lectures given by Heidegger in 1929–30 on the three fundamental concepts of metaphysics: the world, finitude and loneliness.[1] I regard these lectures as one of Heidegger's most impressive philosophical achievements. My aim in presenting his analysis of boredom is not primarily to give an account of Heidegger, but rather to use it to gain a better understanding of how boredom expresses itself and influences experience as a whole.[2] Via these phenomenological investigations, I will also establish a set of premises for chapter Four.

ON ATTUNEMENT[3]

In *Tractatus logico-philosophicus* Wittgenstein states that 'the world of the happy is a different world from the world of the unhappy.'[4] This claim is discussed at greater length in his diaries for 1914–16, where he ends up asking 'Can there be a world which is neither happy nor unhappy?'[5] The answer to this question is far from self-evident, as it depends on how one defines the notions of 'happiness' and 'unhappiness' and whether these are the only alternatives. For there are a number of other moods that do not have to be regarded as variations of happiness and unhappiness.[6] We can reformulate Wittgenstein's question thus: 'Can there be a world that is not characterized by any sort of attunement, any mood?' In this case, I will argue that the answer is a categorical no.

Emotions and moods have, generally speaking, received relatively little attention in philosophy. This is in part due to the traditional distinction between primary and secondary sensory qualities, where primary sensory qualities, such as extension and weight, are taken to be objective, whereas secondary qualities, such as colour and taste, are regarded as subjective. Emotions are almost without exception classified as secondary, or even tertiary, qualities. The only areas in which they have been given due attention is in ethics and aesthetics, while they have generally been left out of epistemology. If emotions and moods can rightly be classified as merely subjective phenomena, their exclusion from epistemology might be in order. However, it is doubtful whether the traditional dichotomy between the strictly subjective and the strictly objective can still be maintained; if not, we must also revise the distinction between primary and secondary qualities.

Can we, for instance, clearly distinguish between whether something *is* boring or if it only *feels* boring? Boredom cannot be placed unambiguously on either the subject- or the object-pole of experience. We seem to be equally justified in holding the *object itself* (a book, a person, a party) to be boring as in merely claiming that the object is boring *for me*. The characteristic 'boredom' is related to both the subject and the object. This holds, by the way, for all other characteristics, seen from a phenomenological point of view. If I, for instance, claim that 'This is a bad car', I appear to be making a merely subjective judgement. However, I can reformulate the judgement as to make it more objective: 'The car breaks down frequently.' This judgement, however, is related to the subject too, because it is fully motivated by the use I intend to make of it.

It is not necessarily any less 'objective' to claim that a book is boring than that it is rectangular and brown.

Boredom is as real as books and protons, even if boredom is a historical phenomenon. Hilary Putnam has persuasively argued that we have to give up the distinction between what 'really' exists in the world and what we merely project into it.[7] From a phenomenological point of view, no clear distinction between the two can be drawn. (Such an assertion will often be met by accusations of unwarrantable idealism, but such accusations are in turn based on an equally unwarrantable idealism.) It is more problematic to pass an 'objective' judgement on the world as a whole, as the world is not an object in the usual sense of the word, more our actual horizon of meaning.

That an observer in a given context can show a greater lack of emotion compared to another, committed observer does not mean that the latter person's judgements are less objective. In a theoretical attitude to objects, i.e., when we attempt to be 'objective', the world comes across as something that lacks meaning.[8] This stems from our effort to reduce everything that lies 'between' ourselves and the things, i.e., their meaning, in order to approach the object as such more directly. This is, of course, only one way of looking at things among many, for to observe an object 'objectively' is only seeing it *as* a certain kind of object. In boredom, our gaze is somewhat similar to the objectivized look, in a purportedly pure perception where music is nothing but a series of sounds and a painting merely blotches of colour. In boredom events and objects are given to us as before, but with the important difference that they appear to have been stripped of meaning. The essential difference between the bored and the 'theoretical' gaze is that the former is the result of an involuntary loss of meaning, while the theoretical gaze deliberately removes it.

It is important to avoid a reduction of moods to strictly psychological phenomena, for then they will appear to throw light solely onto our mental life and not onto the world. Heidegger argues that precisely the fact that we are subject to moods indicates that they are *not* mere inner states that are projected onto a meaningless world. We cannot determine if a mood is something 'interior' or 'exterior' to the subject, as moods go beyond such a distinction and must be taken as a basic characteristic of our being-in-the-world. A change of mood must therefore also be taken as a change in the world – when we operate with a concept of the world as something that can have, or lack, meaning – for we have no un-attuned world to compare it with, a world that would not be affected by the change of mood.

When we are in a joyful mood, *everything* appears to be vibrant and full of life, and when we are sad everything is dull or dead. A mood is always general, affecting the world as a whole. Emotions are not necessarily general. My arachnophobia, for example, is quite specific, as it relates to one particular kind of object: spiders. And when we are angry, we are usually angry with a particular person. There are, however, considerable overlaps, and most of us have experienced being angry at the whole world, because it has apparently treated one badly. Generally speaking, a mood will also extend over a longer period of time than an emotion. An emotion can also often be related to a particular part of the body, while mood cannot. In what part of the body, for example, should one feel boredom? If the emotion is not connected to a particular part of the body, we will be able to relate it to a particular object. As far as my arachnophobia is concerned, I do not single out any part of the body but the spider that causes the fear.[9] Broadly speaking, we can say that an emotion normally has an intentional object, while a mood is objectless. Moods have more to do with the totality of all objects, i.e., the world as a whole. E. M. Cioran has pointed out that 'pain is localised, whereas boredom evokes an evil without any site, without any support, without anything except this nothing, unidentifiable, which erodes you.'[10] I would claim that boredom can be an emotion, but it can also be a mood. It is an emotion when one is bored by something specific and it is a mood when the world as such is boring. We can say that situative boredom is often an emotion, while existential boredom is always a mood. I am mainly interested in the latter.

It is surely uncontroversial to claim that all cognition is conditioned by its context or situation, but a situation also requires a mood in order to be understood as a certain kind of situation. A situation may turn out to be dangerous only if the observer is attuned in such a way that the danger can emerge. Underlying all cognition are interests, and these interests must, in a final analysis, be understood in the light of moods. Perhaps it is most correct to say that we have cognition of a situation by virtue of the mood through which the situation is given to us. A mood is not merely a strictly subjective determination nor is it strictly objective. It is in the actual polarity that exists between humans and their surroundings. It is basically via a mood that we relate to our surroundings.

Being attuned is not merely an ontological determination of man, for it also makes up an *epistemic* condition for how objects can convey meaning in various sorts of ways. A mood makes some experiences possible, others impossible. It conditions how the world – and therefore also all objects and events – appears to us. Otto Friedrich Bollnow has said that 'The mood is the primordial, and only within its bounds and conditioned by it does the perception of a single object follow.' [11] I believe that it is slightly misleading to place the mood as *prior* to the uncovering of the particular objects, as the mood itself is given *with* the cognition of these objects. At the same time, it is clear that the mood is essential for how these objects are perceived. The mood appears to be prior to perception because of its connection to facticity, to already being in the world, but this facticity is revealed simultaneously with the experience of the particular objects in the world. There is a certain primacy to the mood, however, because cognition presupposes an interest that can give it some direction. The mood forms a basic frame for understanding and experience. Different moods give us different experiences of time, but also different experiences of space, as all spaces are attuned.[12] Time and space are interrelated, and in boredom the temporal *horror vacui* also becomes a spatial *horror loci*, where the emptiness of this particular *place* torments me. In the same way as one wants the time to pass in a state of situative boredom, one also wants to escape the place where one is located. And just as time virtually implodes in existential boredom, becoming a kind of eternal and dull present time, all one's surroundings lose their vitality, and the difference between the proximate and the distant collapses.

Not all experiences can be made at will – aesthetic experiences, for instance, or loving somebody. Being grumpy is a mood, and when I am grumpy, even the activities that usually give me joy are just irritating. When in such a mood, there is little point in my going to a concert, because no matter how good the music might be, I will probably be unable to fully take part in the experience. The mood is a condition for experience by opening up the world as a whole. So it is fitting when Beckett (in an early work) talked about a 'transcendental gloom',[13] for a state of melancholy is transcendental or at least quasi-transcendental because it makes possible a certain mode of experience. Experiences become possible by virtue of moods that are suitable for it. Certain moods may incite sociality (e.g., joy), whereas others are more likely to lead to loneliness (e.g., boredom).[14] And just think of when this or that close friend is overcome with sadness and seems withdrawn. S/he no longer takes part in the friendship as s/he used to, and even though it is hard to put one's finger on exactly what has changed, it is as if the entire friendship has altered, because a wall of different attunement has come between you and that person. We are not only attuned separately but often *share* moods, and it seems reasonable to believe that any social group to some extent needs shared moods in order to maintain its existence. I also suppose that the greater extent to which a mood is shared by a group, the less visible the mood will be for the individuals so attuned. Certain moods promote activity, others hinder it. When one is in a mood, the world seems to be a particular field of possibilities;[15] boredom differs from most other moods by the fact that the possibilities withdraw.

One is usually unaware of being attuned in a particular way. It is possible to be bored without knowing it. Cioran describes boredom as 'Pure erosion, the effect of which is imperceptible and which gradually transforms you into a ruin not perceived by others and virtually unperceived by you yourself.'[16] But moods can be recovered, as when Marcel dips his Madeleine cake into his tea in Proust's *Remembrance of Things Past*, or when we notice a certain odour, which for instance is the same as the one in a classroom in primary school, and we suddenly realize that everything we experienced in this room was shrouded in an unmistakeable mood. But we cannot simply through an act of will recover a previous mood, a mood belonging to a time now past. As Proust observed:

> And so it is with our own past. It is a labour in vain to attempt to recapture it: all the efforts of our intellect must prove futile. The past is hidden somewhere outside the realm, beyond the reach of the intellect, in some material object (in the sensation which that material object will give us) of which we have no inkling. And it depends on chance whether or not we come upon this object before we ourselves must die.[17]

Suddenly, through an involuntary act of remembrance, the attunements of the past can be awakened in us.

We are essentially passive in relation to moods, but we can learn to understand them and in this way gain some independence from them. We can also attempt to bring about contrary moods. This is an old theme in philosophy, and Spinoza especially has described how one can transform oneself from being entirely subjected to passive emotions and instead promote active emotions in oneself. One mood can be replaced by another, but it is impossible to leave attunement altogether. However, profound boredom brings us as close to a state of un-attunement as we can come.

Heidegger's concept for the kind of being we ourselves are is *Dasein*. Literally it means 'being-there'. We are the sort of beings who are *there*, in the world. What characterizes *Dasein* is that its existence is a *concern* for it in its existence. An essential aspect of our existence is to have a relation to our own existence. Unlike animals, plants or rocks, *Dasein* always has a self-understanding. This can be one definition of it: *Dasein* is a being that has an understanding of itself in its existence. It is a self-interpreting being. A mood defines *Dasein*'s *there* by opening up the space in which *Dasein* can relate to itself. This mood is more fundamental than the distinction between the inner and the outer. I am *in* a mood, but we can justifiably argue that the mood comes to me from the world. Unlike empiricist and rationalist positions, moods in Heidegger also point to an outside, to *Dasein*'s exposure to the world: 'The mood is precisely the fundamental way in which we are outside of our self.'[18]

By means of an analysis of moods, we attempt to uncover the fundamental affectedness (*Befindlichkeit*) of human existence, i.e., of *how* it is to be in the world. Affectedness is a passive aspect of *Dasein*'s disclosure of the world and itself, and it mainly lies outside *Dasein*'s control. But it is important to emphasise the significance of this affectedness, as it is a necessary condition for *Dasein*'s perception of beings as significant or indifferent. This affectedness reveals itself through moods, and it is therefore most directly the moods that disclose that something has a certain significance for *Dasein*. In affectedness *Dasein* shows itself to be open to the world, and a mood discloses that something in the world, or the world as a whole, has a particular significance for *Dasein*. In affectedness it is shown that *Dasein* is open to the world, that *Dasein* allows itself to be affected, and such an openness is a necessary condition for cognition. Affectedness consists in *Dasein* always already finding itself as situated, and this situatedness is what makes interpretation possible.

Heidegger claims that philosophy always takes place in a fundamental mood.[19] The mood is the condition for, and environment of, all thought and action. It sets thought in action as a condition made by being. *Dasein* always sees its own project through the moods.[20] It is the mood that gets *Dasein* 'in touch' with the world, where 'pure' perception would keep it at a distance. To be attuned is to see the world under an aspect, and the world cannot be seen except as under an aspect. The fundamental mood is more basic than the idea. There is no discursive totality, but rather that which lets the world appear as a totality. Both philosophy and everyday life have a tendency to suppress the attunement,[21] and in everyday life it is also usually suppressed,[22] but it reveals itself in precarious situations.

One of the most objectionable aspects of emphasising attunement is that much of the autonomy of thought must be renounced. Thought now seems to be merely an articulation of and a response to whatever is given with the mood. There is a fundamental passivity in the change to another time than the one being lived in a given situation, and with the opening for reflection. Access to time cannot simply be willed but has to be given to us. Philosophy cannot simply force itself on a phenomenon, but must wait for 'temporalisation of access'.[23] By awakening the mood of boredom, Heidegger believes we will be in position to gain access to time and the meaning of being. For Heidegger, boredom is a privileged fundamental mood because it leads us directly into the very problem complex of being and time.

ONTOLOGY: THE HERMENEUTICS OF BOREDOM

Heidegger is far more famous for his analysis of anxiety than that of boredom. Otto Friedrich Bollnow criticized Heidegger for founding the entire fundamental ontology in one mood only, namely anxiety.[24] This is strange, since Heidegger analyses a great number of moods, whereas Bollnow more or less neglects boredom.[25] As for myself, I must admit that I have never really managed to fully penetrate Heidegger's analysis of anxiety, presumably simply because I have not all that much experience of anxiety. I also notice this when I lecture on Heidegger. Anxiety seems to be virtually unknown to the students, while things are very different with boredom. Boredom simply seems to be a more contemporary phenomenon than anxiety. We no longer suffer as much from anxiety, but all the more from boredom. Or to put it more in Heideggerian terms: Anxiety is no longer as anxious, but boredom is increasingly bored.

Heidegger writes about the necessity of awaking a fundamental mood for philosophizing, and something that must be awakened is already present, but lies *sleeping*.[26] One must be *awakened* to seize a fundamental mood. Heidegger wants to awaken boredom rather than let it slumber through various forms of everyday pastime (*Zeitvertrieb*). That seems undeniably to be an odd ambition – after all, we usually combat boredom, and if it 'sleeps' we should be satisfied with that. The reason why Heidegger wants to awaken boredom is that he believes that we are also 'asleep' in our everyday pastimes in our actual life. This is a far more destructive sleep because it conceals the true possibilities we have. The main problem with actual life is that it does not give us access to the grounds of existence because it is a life 'fleeing from the fundamental'.[27] 'Living is caring – especially in the sense of making-it-easy-for-oneself, fleeing.'[28] The world I care for covers me up. And Heidegger wants to generate '*Dasein*'s vigilance for itself'.[29] Certain existential situations, such as anxiety and boredom, open up for a counter-movement because *Dasein* in these situations no longer can rely on the world but is brutally thrown back on itself.[30]

According to Heidegger there are various forms of boredom, ranging from the superficial to the one that reaches the very ground of Being, but even the merely superficial form of boredom has a potential because it can lead us to profound boredom: 'This *superficial* boredom is even meant to lead us to *profound* boredom, or, to put it more appropriately, the superficial boredom is supposed to manifest itself as the profound boredom and to attune us through and through in the ground of *Dasein*. This fleeting, cursory, *inessential* boredom must become *essential*.'[31] Our investigation of boredom requires very little from us in order to begin. It is enough not to resist the boredom that already exists and give it room to affect one. However, this simple procedure is far from easy to follow. So we should perhaps rather focus on the activities we engage in while attempting to avoid boredom – our devotion to everyday pastimes.

To while away the time is an attempt to drive away boredom by finding something or other – in principle, it can be anything that can hold one's attention. When we are bored, we usually look at a watch, and this differs from shifting one's position in a chair or letting one's eyes wander, because looking at a watch simply does not function as a pastime. It is rather just a sign of our wish to while away time, or more precisely 'our failure to pass the time, and thus indicates that we are *becoming increasingly bored*.'[32] Watching the clock indicates that boredom is increasing. We look at the watch wishing to see that time has passed, that it has gone faster than it felt like, that the lecture will soon be over, that the train will soon arrive, etc. But we are usually disappointed. At the same time, it is worth noting that it is not the objectively measurable length of the watch's time that is linked to boredom, because it is not the length but rather the pace of time that is of importance. The watch always moves at exactly the same pace. The strictly quantitative aspects of time are clearly not crucial for boredom, and looking at the watch should therefore be an irrelevant act. In boredom, time is slow, and because of this slowness we notice that we are not in charge of time, that we are subject to time. We attempt to drive away this power by means of our everyday pastimes. We let our gaze wander, not looking for anything in particular, but for anything that can fill our gaze. Ernst Jünger describes the boredom he experienced when lying wounded in a field hospital: 'When one lies there bored, one looks for distractions in many different ways. Thus I once lay passing the time by counting my wounds.'[33] Considering the number of times Jünger was wounded, this should certainly have kept him occupied for quite a while. He probably also counted the number of light bulbs hanging from the ceiling and other things. Exactly what one counts is of relative unimportance. Strictly speaking, the pastime has no object because what concerns us is not the activity or object we are occupied with, but rather the occupation itself. We seek to be occupied because it liberates us from the emptiness of boredom. When we manage to stay fully occupied, time disappears in favour of whatever fills it.

What do we mean by describing time as empty? Despite everything, it always has a certain content, no matter how 'thin' that may be, and we can be completely absorbed by some minute detail. So it must be primarily a question of what *relation* one has to its content. It is neither time itself nor what fills it as such that give us an answer as to the origin of boredom. For Heidegger, 'A boring thing is one which belongs to a boring situation.' [34] This apparently tautological formulation is not as empty as it appears to be at first glance, because the important notion of a *situation* is brought into the discussion. It is not time itself or the things themselves, but the situation in which they are placed that can give rise to boredom. In certain situations the things that surround us do not seem to offer us anything. Exactly what should they offer? When we wait at an airport, we get information about arrivals and departures, we can buy sandwiches, a cup of coffee, slip into the smokers' lounge, read newspapers . . . So why is waiting at airports so deadly boring, when airports actually provide so many possibilities for whiling away the time? The answer is that an airport often denies us the possibility we want most of all – to get on a plane at the scheduled time so we can leave the airport itself. The airport is only there to be left. For me, when delays occur, my total situation at the airport differs from the situation when everything runs on schedule, and this change of situation creates a different experience of time. 'Boredom is possible at all only because each thing, as we say, has *its* time. If each thing did not have its own time, there would be no boredom.' [35] Hence, boredom arises when there is a discrepancy between the thing's own time and the time in which we encounter the thing. This is a tentative answer to the question as to the essence of boredom.

Heidegger then investigates whether there is a more profound form of boredom that can lead us closer to the very origin of the phenomenon. He makes a distinction between 'being bored with something' (*Gelangweiltwerden von etwas*) and 'boring oneself with something' (*Sichlangweilen bei etwas*), the second a more profound form of boredom.[36] In the first form we know what is boring us, namely the airport or the lecture. This is what has previously been referred to as situative boredom, where what is boring is fairly unambiguous. It is more difficult to find a good example of the second form, precisely because the boring is not as unambiguously defined. Heidegger's example is that of being invited to a dinner party where the food is good, as is the music, and the guests are enjoying one other's company. I am at this party. Before I realize it, the party is over and I walk home. Once back home, I am struck by the thought that I was actually bored the entire evening. This is presumably an experience most of us have had at some time. The strange thing about this form of boredom is that I am unable to identify exactly what I was bored with. I did not make a single attempt during the entire evening to while the time away; on the contrary, I gave time free rein. And yet it feels as if the whole evening was nothing more than just passing the time. At a closer scrutiny, the party as such was a mere pastime. The boredom and the pastime coincide. The pastime did not take place within a situation – the pastime itself *was* the situation. That is precisely why this pastime was less visible and why it normally takes place without our noticing that we are mainly dealing with a pastime. The consciousness of boredom that sometimes strikes us afterwards should be understood as a consciousness of an emptiness. Even though the party was pleasant and entertaining, it was completely empty. I did not look at my watch once or long for the party to end. I wholeheartedly attempted to fulfil my role as a guest and did not let my attention wander. What was the emptiness that struck me when I got home? According to Heidegger, the emptiness that crops up in this more profound form of boredom is the emptiness left by 'our proper self'.[37] In spite of time apparently being filled to the brim, there was still an emptiness, which means that my activities failed to fulfil my needs. We could perhaps say that the situation was not meaning-full. What strikes me is the thought that I should make more of my life than just be a guest at dinner parties.

At the party I was fully occupied with whatever happened in my surroundings. In this total simultaneity I was cut off from my past and future in favour of a present that filled the entire time horizon.[38] Some people will perhaps argue that living in the present is a good thing, but I can relate to the present in authentic and inauthentic ways. In order for the relation to be authentic, i.e., be an expression of my true self, it must be related to my past and future, to who I was cast into the world as and to the projections I make for the future. But I can also relate to the present in such a way as to interpret myself almost exclusively in terms of whatever happens to surround me in a given situation, thereby letting the situation define who I am. The more profound boredom is characterized by the situation itself being the pastime, and the boredom therefore does not have its origin *in* the situation, Heidegger claims, but must be sought in *Dasein* itself: 'The boredom springs from the temporality of *Dasein*.'[39] This means that it originates in the temporalization of temporality, in how *Dasein*'s temporality unfolds itself. I believe this to be a weak point in Heidegger's analysis. Even though the boredom does not stem from anything specific in a given situation, it can stem from the surroundings understood as a more comprehensive context. So it is not strictly necessary to seek recourse to *Dasein*'s own temporality at this point in the analysis. However, I will disregard this objection for the sake of the argument.

Heidegger now moves on to a third form of boredom, which is the truly profound one. He claims that the more profound the boredom is, the more profoundly it is rooted in the temporality one's self is.[40] In the profound form of boredom, I am bored by boredom itself – I am completely attuned by boredom. 'The profound boredom bores when we say, or rather when we silently know, *it is* boring for one (*es ist einem langweilig*).'[41] What is meant by this 'it' that is boring for one? It is the same 'it' as you can find in expressions like 'it is snowing', 'it is raining', etc. If someone were to ask you what this 'it' is that is snowing or raining, you would be pushed for an answer, for 'it' is something unknown or unspecific. It is always possible to nominalize and say 'the snowing snows' or 'the raining rains', and thus make tautologies. Heidegger opts for this solution, as so often in his writings, even going so far as to argue that phenomenology in its essence is tautological.[42] Hence, his answer to the question as to what bores us is: the Boring (*das Langweilende*). It is not I who bore myself, or you who bore yourself but the Boring that bores one. For such a boredom all personal characteristics – age, gender, profession, endless other personal characteristics – are irrelevant. It is a boredom that goes beyond all of this. In the superficial form of boredom, one is left empty by the objects around one, but in profound boredom, one is left empty by everything – even by oneself. Heidegger cannot find any illustrating example for this form of boredom, precisely because it is not related to any specific situation, as the previous named forms of boredom are. Our task now is to understand this boredom in its 'might', as it 'reveals the state we are in':

> Whereas in the first case of boredom we are concerned to shout down the boredom by passing the time so we do not need to listen to it; and whereas in the second case what is distinctive is a not wanting to listen, we now have a being compelled to listen, being compelled in the sense of that compelling force which everything properly authentic about *Dasein* possesses, and which accordingly is related to *Dasein*'s innermost freedom . . . [43]

At first sight, it might seem strange to relate coercion and inner freedom in such a way, but Heidegger's point is that one is forced to take one's own freedom into account instead of attempting to forget it while engaging in various pastimes.

How does boredom force us to do this? By depriving us of everything by making it indifferent, in such a way that we cannot find a foothold anywhere. The things do not lose their significance one by one – everything collapses into one indifferent whole.

> We are not merely relieved of our everyday personality, somehow distant and alien to it, but simultaneously also elevated beyond the particular situation in each case and beyond the specific beings surrounding us there. The whole situation and we ourselves as this individual subject are thereby indifferent, indeed this boredom does not even let it get to the point where such things are of any particular worth to us.[44]

Dasein is handed over to a whole of being that withdraws itself. This negatively indicates *Dasein*'s genuine possibilities that lie fallow in boredom. Everything becomes both indifferent and bothersome in its lack of meaning. This indifference also characterizes me. I become an empty 'nobody' who can be experienced in my emptiness. In a sense it would be most correct to claim that *Nobody* is bored or that boredom is bored. For Heidegger, this is precisely what makes a radical turn possible, because the self is brought to a naked encounter with itself, as the self that is *there* and is left to its own devices. This outermost and first possibility makes possible all possibilities of *Dasein*.[45] It is not a possibility related to my person as such, i.e., my ontic determinations – because they have become indifferent in boredom – but to what makes anything at all possible for me.

In boredom *Dasein* is imprisoned in time, but an imprisoned *Dasein* can also be liberated – by opening up to itself. *Dasein*'s process of liberation takes place by *Dasein* seizing its own possibilities and bringing all of time together in *the moment* (*der Augenblick*). 'The moment of vision is nothing other than the look of resolute disclosedness (*Blick der Entschlossenheit*), in which in the full situation of an action opens itself and keeps itself open.'[46] In the moment, time enables possibilities. A break with the time of boredom is opened up. Heidegger is referring here to Kierkegaard's concept of the moment (*Øjeblikket*), as he also does in *Sein und Zeit*. It should, however, be noted that Heidegger dismisses Kierkegaard's concept as based on a vulgar notion of time,[47] and I think that it would be more fruitful here to introduce St Paul's concept *kairos*, for Heidegger also translates this by *Augenblick* in German. St Paul makes considerable use of metaphors connected to sleeping and waking. Here are two typical examples: 'We shall not all sleep, but we shall all be changed in a moment.';[48] 'And that, knowing the time, know it is high time to awake out of sleep: for now is our salvation nearer than when we believed.'[49]

Here is a third: 'Therefore let us not sleep, as do others; but let us watch and be sober.'[50] For Heidegger, 'us' would be synonymous with the actual thinkers, while 'the others' are all those who have not yet gained philosophical insight. But the select company is, in principle, open to all.[51] Heidegger wants to regain the Christian fundamental experiences and the 'fullness of time' mentioned in the 'Epistle to the Galatians',[52] but he wants to replace Christ by temporality: 'The Christian experience lives time as such.'[53] For Paul the *parousia* refers to Christ's Second Coming, an event that must be waited for in a moment (*kairos*) of vigilance. The early Christians rejected *kronos*, the mundane time of the calendar, in favour of the moment in which true insight and revelation take place, and thereby experience the specific historical situation. For Heidegger, *kairos* and *parousia* become one and the same, and the goal is to be vigilant as regards one's own self. Vigilance, where *kairos* not *kronos* is time, defines authenticity. *Kairos* is connected to *krisis*, the decision or resolution to turn from *kronos* to *kairos*. *Parousia* finds its genuine expression in an experience of Being as original temporality in the moment, where

Dasein chooses its own possibilities. In *Sein und Zeit* Heidegger describes the 'unshakeable joy' and 'sober anxiety' that characterize *Dasein* in actuality.[54] Given the general proximity between the analyses of boredom and anxiety, there is reason to believe that authenticity will be characterized by a 'sober boredom' and a calm joy. But the road to such a condition *has* to be hard. Heidegger makes one think here of some lines in a poem by Federico García Lorca:

No one sleeps in the sky. No one, no one.
No one sleeps.
But if someone should close his eyes,
whip him, my sons, whip him!

There will be a landscape of open eyes
and bitter fiery wounds.[55]

Heidegger sees himself as our saviour – or at least as the messenger of salvation – as the one who is to lead us into and then out of a boredom of such profundity that we will be brought to grasp our own possibilities for being. Heidegger's analysis aims at transforming the reader in such a way as to bring out an essential dimension of existence from its hiding place.

We have now, in a way, reached the end-point of Heidegger's phenomenology of boredom, the point at which boredom is so radical as to be able to bring about a turn-around to authenticity. *Dasein*, then, exists (*ek-stasis* = stands out) in an field of authentic possibilities. However, a weakness with the presentation so far is that it has given the impression that boredom is an ahistorical entity that belongs to the essence of *Dasein*. Admittedly, boredom belongs to the essence of *Dasein* as a *possibility* – because *Dasein* is time and boredom is one possible expression of time – but Heidegger also believes that boredom, as a fundamental mood, is *typical* for the people of his time. Why is that? Because *Dasein* no longer has an essential need of anything:

> The absence of an essential oppressiveness in *Dasein* is the emptiness as a whole, so that no one stands with anyone else and no community stands with any other in the rooted unity of essential action. Each and every one of us are servants of slogans, adherents to a program, but none is the custodian of the inner greatness of *Dasein* and its necessities (*Bedrängnis*). This being left empty (*Leergelassenheit*) ultimately resonates in our *Dasein*, its emptiness is the absence of any essential oppressiveness. The mystery is lacking in our *Dasein*, and thereby the inner terror that every mystery carries with it and that gives *Dasein* its greatness remains absent.[56]

Heidegger's point is that we have all become isolated individuals who are subject to impersonal, abstract notions, and no longer feel any strong need for anything, or for doing anything essential; life has, in a sense, simply become too easy. This lightness is the source of boredom, and this lightness becomes a pretext for doing nothing, allowing *Dasein* to forget the task of becoming what it essentially is. In *Sein und Zeit* Heidegger is eager to try to show that the experience of anxiety makes possible a freer, more authentic relation to oneself. Profound boredom also provides such a possibility, but there is reason to believe that it demands more of a personal effort to exploit the latent possibilities. One can slumber into boredom, but hardly into anxiety. That is why waking boredom is so crucial for Heidegger, for him to demonstrate its radical nature, to make existence more difficult: 'Only those who can truly give themselves a burden are free.'[57] One possible burden is philosophy, as philosophy takes place in the 'fundamental attunement of melancholy' (*Schwermut*).[58]

In several places, Heidegger emphasises that the metaphysical questions can arise only on the basis of a fundamental mood. A fundamental mood must be awakened in order to open up a metaphysical questioning that reveals oneself as a metaphysical subject in a world. Boredom can therefore be an initiation to metaphysics.[59] The two extremities of metaphysics are present in boredom: the world as a whole *and* the individual, linked by their relationship to the same nothingness. Philosophy is born in the nothingness of boredom. Boredom reveals an emptiness, an insignificance, where all things are drawn into an all-compassing indifference. Boredom arises from the preoccupation with mere things in inauthentic, everyday life. Inauthentic *Dasein* 'has no time' because the fundamental movement towards the things in the world removes time by filling it so completely that it disappears into pure transparency.[60] The temporality of everyday life causes the indifference in the world it discloses and it thereby creates boredom. In everydayness, things are given to us with 'remarkable undifferentiatedness'.[61] This must not be taken to mean that we do not make distinctions between things, for we are constantly searching for something new and different. The lack of difference must rather be understood as a flatness, meaning that we do not approach the things as essential things. As Heidegger puts it, *Dasein* 'cannot see the world for the things'.[62]

Dasein stiffens in everydayness – and in the world. Boredom is to reveal this stiffness. In boredom one is caught in a vortex of immanence, where *Dasein* is no longer genuinely ec-static, i.e. transcending. Boredom is reminiscent of eternity, where there is no transcendence. Time collapses, implodes, into a vast, empty present. Time is usually transparent – we do not take any notice of it – and it does not appear as a something. But in our confrontation with a nothing in boredom, where time is not filled with anything that can occupy our attention, we experience time as time.

As Joseph Brodsky puts it, boredom 'represents pure, undiluted time in all its redundant, monotonous splendour.'[63] In boredom, time becomes 'refractory' because it will not pass like it usually does, and this is why the reality of time can be experienced. The meaning of human life collapses. The relationship of *Dasein* to the world disappears, and what remains is a nothing, an all-compassing lack. *Dasein* is trapped in time, abandoned in an emptiness that seems impossible to fill. *Dasein* is bored because life lacks a purpose and a meaning – and the task of boredom is to draw our attention to precisely this.

Boredom is dehumanizing by depriving human life of the meaning that constitutes it as a life. We can hardly imagine what animal life is like in any other way than viewing it as somewhat similar to human life, but poorer, as a world with less meaning. In boredom there is a loss of world. *Dasein* becomes world-impoverished (*weltarm*). In this sense, one seems to approach a state of animal existence in boredom – but can animals be bored? It would seem to be undeniable that, for example, dogs can appear to be bored at times, but I believe that such an attribution of boredom to an animal is normally nothing more than anthropomorphism. To be bored one must be able to be aware of a lack of meaning – or at least be able later to be aware of the fact that one was bored on a particular occasion because the situation was boring. The analogy between human boredom and animal existence breaks down because animals cannot suffer a loss of meaning, as they have no relation to experience in the first place. It is therefore quite misleading to make any comparison between boredom and animality, because there is an 'abyss' between these two types of existence.[64] Is it the awareness of a loss of meaning (or forgetting of being) that makes *Dasein* what it is, that distinguishes it from the purely animal? It would be imprecise to claim anything of the kind, for *Dasein* is more fundamentally defined via an understanding of being, no matter how covert that might be. Animals lack the 'as-structure' in experience.[65] They do not see anything *as* anything, but live in an unmediated continuum with their surroundings.

Human existence, on the other hand, is constituted as a being-in-the-world, where there is a polarity between human and world. Being-in-the-world contains, or *is*, such a polarity between subject and object. Over-zealous disciples of Heidegger argue that he went beyond the very subject–object dichotomy, but he of course only overcame a certain conception of such a dichotomy. The point is that the relation between subject and object must be understood as having an in-between, and it is in this very in-between, in the polarity between the two, that meaning can arise. If we are to place moods anywhere, they will also have to be placed in this in-between, as they make up an essential part of our *relation* to the world. Otto Friedrich Bollnow describes the mood in anxiety and despair as broken or shattered (*zerbrochen*).[66] This also serves well as a description of boredom, where the meaning-conveying polarity is gone. Boredom is mood which is reminiscent of an absence of moods. Since the mood is essential for our relation to objects, and boredom is a kind of non-mood, our relation to things also becomes a kind of non-relation.

In *Dasein* there is a tendency towards falling into the world, for letting life pass by as a serious of inauthentic diversions. Heidegger attempts to uncover what evokes a sense of terror in us.[67] We are to be scared awake by letting boredom be awakened in us. *Dasein* is not at home in the world of boredom. The world has become uncanny or unhomely (*unheimlich*) – it is threatening and no longer appears to be a comforting home. In boredom we experience the reality of nothingness, or rather the nothingness of reality. Things slip away and our normal relation to them breaks down. The nothingness of boredom seems ultimately to be the only phenomenon that has relevance for us. Boredom removes a veil of meaning from things and allows them to appear as empty and ephemeral. Exactly what remains then? Nothing less than Being. Even fully immersed in nothingness, *Dasein is* still there, and Being can then reveal itself to *Dasein*. The inauthentic mode of being covers up the true character of one's being. By shattering inauthentic *Dasein*'s frictionless relation to the world, we are to be awakened into an authentic relation to ourselves. Actual life is never sovereignly self-moving,[68] but it can reach a higher degree of freedom than it has in average everydayness. By means of the breakdown of all meaning, *Dasein* is to be freed from its dependence upon mere beings.

However, is there not a problem with Heidegger's analysis as to how one moves from a pre-philosophical (unauthentic) to a philosophical (authentic) standpoint? Heidegger believes that philosophy can counteract the fallenness to which *Dasein* necessarily is subject. But if the impetus towards the world, the falling, is so strong and belongs to the very essence of *Dasein*, one wonders how Heidegger's own analysis is possible. Does not his analysis presuppose that a contrary movement, a counter-corruption (*Gegenruinanz*), is already in operation? What might the source for such a counter-corrupting movement be?

While boredom ultimately detaches one completely both from the world and oneself, it is supposed in its most radical form to have the resources for a contrary movement. From where do these resources stem? Does not Heidegger silently presuppose a potent Nietzschean will deep inside, Cartesian remains of substantiality, a solid point for which no phenomenological evidence has been provided? Can we believe in Heidegger's potent *Dasein*? Even if *Dasein* loses the support from all other beings, it is supposed to have the resources within for a restoration of itself. Is not this only yet another version of the Romantic paradigm? Boredom contains a need or longing for a different time, and Heidegger identifies this time with *kairos*. Is Heidegger really on the *track* of a lost time, or does this other time only stand there as an assertion? It is characteristic that Heidegger never completed his analysis of time, where the three temporal ecstasies of past, present and future were to have been united in one temporality. In a way, time is left as a utopian idea, as merely promised potential.

Heidegger claims that boredom 'grows from the depths'.[69] Consequently, this boredom must be 'deep' in the sense of being profound. But what is so 'profound' about boredom? Doesn't Heidegger commit a highly questionable sublimation of boredom? There is a constant tendency in Heidegger to rewrite everything that is low, dirty, painful or evil as some-thing grand, namely as being an expression of *Being*. Why is it so crucial to make boredom grand? Presumably because Heidegger is convinced that grand people are attuned by grand moods whereas small people are merely attuned by small moods or whims.[70] A common, 'low' boredom simply does not appear to carry enough significance to uphold the great philosophical onus that Heidegger wishes to place on it. Heidegger is unwilling to accept the commonness of human life, and he is therefore constantly in danger of overlooking the ontic (beings) in favour of the ontological (Being).

The reason why Heidegger's analysis of boredom takes such a turn is that all other questions are subordinated to the question of Being or 'the meaning of Being'. After studying Heidegger's philosophy for a number of years, I have come to the conclusion that the question of Being is not a genuine question, that there is no 'Being as such', and that Heidegger's project was therefore doomed to fail.[71] When we renounce the notion of 'Being as such', we are once more left with a variety of meanings regarding the notion of 'being'. Being bored is one mode of being among others. Precisely because there is no 'Being as such', boredom cannot be elevated or reduced to merely being an expression of Being, but must rather be recognized as a separate phenomenon. Boredom is admittedly related to a great number of other phenomena, but all these phenomena are *co-ordinated*, side by side, rather than placed in a hierarchy. Boredom is nothing more than one phenomenon in human existence. Heidegger constructs a monumental boredom that is supposed to disclose the full meaning and significance of human existence and thereby encourage a turn-around to authenticity. Only a grand mood, an abysmal boredom, can manage such an assignment. But Heidegger thereby loses sight of human existence as it really is, and it was this actual life that he originally set out to investigate.

Heidegger believes that boredom can be overcome, and that is precisely his mistake – he remains within the logic of transgression. He recognizes that boredom indicates a commitment we have to the way we live our lives, but he wrongly believes that this commitment requires that one renounces this entire way of living. In my opinion, though, this commitment is one to the life we live here and now. The commitment is a commitment to the concrete, not to Being. And this commitment includes the necessity of accepting boredom, rather than an attempt to overcome it.

For Heidegger Being is what makes boredom 'profound', but boredom is not so 'profound' – not at least in the way Heidegger presumes. In the following chapter I argue that boredom can be a source for genuine insight by creating a space for reflection, but this insight does not have as wide-reaching ontological implications as Heidegger presupposes. Boredom does not lead us to any profound, encompassing understanding of 'the meaning of Being', but it can tell us something about how we actually lead our lives. This might not be enough for Heidegger, but it is all the phenomenon has to offer.

FOUR

The Ethics of Boredom

The title of this chapter is potentially misleading. It suggests that I intend to put forward a set of practical precepts as to how one ought to view boredom. This is not my intention. There is no solution to the problem of boredom – that is what makes it a problem. The title can, however, be understood to imply that I feel that boredom has its own moral. That is closer to the truth. I do not believe that boredom as a phenomenon can be a platform for any substantial moral philosophy, but I do believe that it has something to tell us about how we live. So it is up to the individual to adopt a stance towards that.

WHAT IS AN I?

I am the sum of all transgressions of myself, i.e., of all that I *do*. What I do is not exterior to who I am; rather, it can be said to be the most explicit expression of who I am. As long as these transgressions function satisfactorily, this is me – so far as I know. If I find a combination I can live with, I will not deviate much from it as long as the outer conditions remain more or less the same. If it is an unsatisfactory combination, or if the outer conditions undergo considerable change, I will seek new transgressions. Life will then become a search for ever-new experiences – and today there are an almost unlimited number on offer. It may also be that I find something unsatisfactory about the perspective of trans-gression itself and ask *why* I am doing all that I do.

With this 'why' I enter into a new relationship with myself. Why have I sought these transgressions? Why have the transgressions formed the constellation they have? I look for a reason as to why I am the person I am. In doing so, I presuppose that there *is* a reason I can derive from all the transgressions. But this reason I am simply unable to find. In my disappointment at not finding any reason I will probably return to the transgression. I can, however, continue to reflect on the reason – or rather on its absence. What I then find is not a reason of any sort but an imprecise feeling that appears to be something that has always been with me. It is as if this feeling is *me*. When I think about it, I have been aware of this feeling for as long as I can remember, and it seems to give me a different perspective on who I am than the perspective of transgression did. This second perspective, though, does not give me any solid ground under my feet. It is, rather, an experiencing of myself as grounded in something unfounded, something that shows that the reason I initially sought for all the transgressions is an abyss, or non-reason. The fundamental is more contingent that what has been founded. There is no original reason that defines who I 'really' am and that can give me any clear answer as to how I ought to live.

Clearly, this 'educational journey' has not produced the desired result. What is to be done, then? Nothing else than to continue. To return to everyday life. To continue as one has always done. To go on, despite the fact one cannot go on. To go on in *now*, where neither past nor future seem to offer any basis for where one ought to go. To go on without any history – or reason – that would indicate any unequivocal direction or overall meaning. To go on in a contemporaneity that has neither beginning nor end.

Perhaps there is something fundamentally mistaken about using boredom as a privileged phenomenon for understanding ourselves and the age we live in. Perhaps we are past boredom. Perhaps time now passes so quickly that it will swallow up boredom or make it imperceptible. As Milan Kundera writes in *Slowness*: 'Speed is the form of ecstasy that humanity has been given by the technical revolution.'[1] And in this speed we can forget ourselves, and perhaps forget that we have lived at all: 'The degree of slowness is directly proportional to the intensity of memory; the degree of speed is directly proportional to the intensity of forgetting.'[2] And those who become philosophers are perhaps those who are a bit slow, who do not forget so easily, who then remember all too well – or at least believe that they remember. Wittgenstein makes such a connection: 'In the race of philosophy, the one who wins is the one who can run slowest. Or: the one who reaches the finishing line last.'[3]

Our concepts of reality and experience are unclear because we have defined them negatively on the basis of an unclear idea of a lack. Is there anything at all that has been lost? Have we lost anything essential, whether we talk about what is lost as time or an experience – which is basically one and the same thing? An awareness of a crucial loss becomes undeniably a principal motif of twentieth-century philosophy (in Adorno, Benjamin, Heidegger and Wittgenstein, for example), and for many of us it was precisely such an awareness of loss that caused us to take up philosophy in the first place. This last-mentioned displays a touching faith in philosophy, but do more than a very few of us still believe that philosophy is able to bring about any salvation?

Because the longed-for presence in the world is always postponed, it is converted into an absence. It is as if all reflection is spurred on by a sentimental look into a nostalgic rear-view mirror. It is a Messianism tapped from Judaism or Christianity where one waits for the First or Second Coming of the Messiah – with the one difference that we have replaced the Messiah by more secular entities, such as an experience or a time. This is a hope that is perhaps too great and that therefore creates an absence, an emptiness. We anticipate metaphysical worries, based on an absence we perhaps are just taking for granted. The meaning we seek in the absence of meaning, the experience in the absence of experience and time in the absence of time – are they merely illusions? An awareness of loss does not guarantee that anything has actually been lost, and therefore does not guarantee either that there is something – a time, meaning or experience – that has to be won back. The title of Proust's masterpiece, *À la recherche du temps perdu*, presupposes that there once was another time, but that this can obviously be self-deception.

Or take such a concept as *alienation*, which practically no one talks about today. Such an expression is only meaningful to the extent that it can be contrasted with a state of participation, identification or unity, because the concept of alienation itself does not express anything except a lack of such a state.[4] Why does no one talk about alienation any more? Two obvious possible answers are: Alienation no longer exists, and consequently there is no use for such a concept; Alienation has become so widespread that we longer have anything with which we can contrast it – the absence of such an absence has become total. What the correct answer is remains unclear. It is, however, clear that a society that lacks social substance, in the Hegelian sense, is not a society one can be alienated from. Are we without alienation and without history?

I am not going to assert that history is over once and for all, for it seems to stop and start at regular intervals. But it is no longer any *great* history that can offer us a monumental meaning into which our lives can be integrated.[5] If history appears to be over, it is because, like our individual lives, it no longer seems to be moving towards any goal. We feel that if the world had a goal, it must already have been achieved,[6] but we do not know what that goal could be. Modernity did, however, manage to wrest itself free of the 'deadweight' of tradition and thereby the present was no longer bound by the past. This liberation, though, did not lead to our freely being able to turn our gaze to the future; it meant, rather, that we were left once more suspended in the lack of absent past, in the experience of loss that is not recognized as anything else than loss. The present time replaced history as the source of meaning, but pure contemporaneity, without any link to past and present, does not give very much meaning. Since we can hardly regain the past as a past, and therefore cannot regain the future as a future either, the task must be to try to establish as substantial a relationship as possible to the present.

The age of nihilism coincided with the heyday of modern philosophy. Nihilism gave philosophy the greatest possibility to establish a world, or rather to save a world in decline. Precisely the vacuum that nihilism created gave philosophy a space to fill. In an interview in 1993, Ernst Jünger said that he considered nihilism as over and done with.[7] It is possible he is right about that, but it is scarcely a basis for saying that philosophy has conquered nihilism. It would be truer to say that in that case nihilism has conquered itself without any new gods arriving on the scene. The present situation is not a 'happy apocalypse', which was Hermann Broch's diagnosis of Vienna at the turn of the twentieth century.[8] This is no apocalypse at all, rather a 'brave new world' – a 'utopia' that has been realized. There can hardly be any new utopias. To the extent that we can imagine a utopia, it must already have been realized. A utopia cannot, by definition, include boredom, but the 'utopia' we are living in is *boring*. Oswald Spengler went so far as to claim that boredom, even in a utopia that had only partly been realized, would be so strong that it would 'lead to mass murder and collective suicide'.[9] On closer inspection, all utopias seem to be deadly boring, because only that which is imperfect is interesting. It is boring to read about utopias, and they all appear to be boring. Novalis asked: 'How can one avoid boredom in the representation of Perfection?'[10] And Pascal underlined that it is not a good thing to have all one's needs satisfied.[11] The utopia we are living in can satisfy practically any need. The utopia does not lack anything – except meaning. When this meaning is looked for, the utopia begins to crack. In his strange novel *Le rivage des Syrtes* (1951), Julien Gracq wrote about the disintegration of a stagnating small society and its way towards war, explaining this by saying 'Ennui descended on everything that for a long time had felt too good'.[12] And Tocqueville wrote about the 'strange melancholy which often haunts the inhabitants of democratic countries in the midst of their abundance.'[13] Boredom constitutes a boundary for a utopia. A utopia can never be completely accomplished, for that would be synonymous with boredom – and this boredom would eat up any utopia from the inside.

THE EXPERIENCE OF BOREDOM

A cure that has often been recommended for boredom is to establish a relationship to God. We saw this very clearly in the case of Pascal. That this is no certain cure, however, was something the early monks already knew, for the premodern precursor of boredom, *acedia*, afflicted monks in particular – and they had devoted their lives to God. Moreover, a long time has passed since God was deposed as a meaning-giving authority, especially during the Enlightenment, which sought to emancipate us and in doing so contributed greatly to the completion of what Adam and Eve began by eating fruit of the Tree of Knowledge.

For us Romantics, work will also appear to be more of a source of boredom than a cure, for the adventurousness of Romanticism was not least a reaction to the monotony of the bourgeois world and its work ethic. This is extremely evident in Friedrich Schlegel's novel *Lucinde* (1799), in the chapter 'The Idyll of Leisure'.[14] Here Schlegel writes in favour of leisure, since 'all the empty, restless activity does not produce anything else than boredom – other people's and one's own.'[15] This ideal of leisure might seem to contradict Romantic striving, but it is directed against the mechanization of man in a modern, bourgeois society, and Schlegel is here putting leisure forward as an alternative to this. He even goes so far as to claim that the 'highest, most fulfilled form of life would then be nothing else than *pure vegetating*.'[16] This, of course, makes one think of Warhol's wish to become a machine, for neither machines nor vegetables are tormented by a spiritual life. But the similarity is only apparent. Schlegel's leisure has a purpose. It is a question of finding tranquillity in a higher longing, and a longing in this tranquillity – a longing that is renewed every time it is fulfilled.[17] We are talking about love. In love the world will once more be animated and acquire substance. Schlegel emphasises in *Lucinde* that Romantic striving needs a goal, that an abstract, endless striving is insufficient. Only love gives his novel's main characters, Julius and Lucinde, a meaningful world beyond boredom. The problem is that an out-and-out infinity, here in Lucinde, is still an infinity. Lucinde becomes a utopian point where Julius can gain reconciliation with the world, but Lucinde is then only a surrogate for God – as woman often is in Romantic poetry – and love becomes just as unattainable as God.[18] And is making a woman or a man a substitute for God in one's life not doing the person concerned a grave injustice? It is to assign a role to them that they are doomed not to be able to fulfil. It also means shirking one's responsibility for boredom, 'passing the buck' to someone else. It is difficult to see all-consuming love as a credible answer to the problem of boredom, for true love will never be able to bear a whole life on its own. Love may seem to be enough when one does not possess it, but when one has, it will always be insufficient.

For Schopenhauer, the answer lay in relinquishing the individual self through aesthetic experience – especially music. Since this relinquishing of the self is hard to achieve for practically all of us – and it most certainly was for Schopenhauer himself – we must, according to him, minimalize our expectations and abandon demands for satisfaction that are too great. Apart from that, aesthetic bliss is always extremely temporary, something Schopenhauer was fully aware of. I doubt that *an aesthetic* revelation, when it comes to it, differs essentially from a chemical, *anaesthetic* revelation. Drugs always stop working, as does music. An intelligent illustration of this point can be found in modern pop music in the Pet Shop Boys. Pop music is based on the banalities of everyday life, and it attempts to convert these banalities in such a way that they make a break possible with everyday boredom. In pop music a hope is formulated that these banalities can become something more. For example, that a form of love exists that can release us from life's heavy burdens or burdensome lightness. And in the absence of this release, pop music can remove some of the excess time, for 'there's still time to kill' (*Up Against It*). As long as the music lasts, we escape boredom, but, sooner or later, the music will stop. In the absence of meaning, the club becomes a place of refuge, and in dancing, embraced by the music, we gain a foretaste of a kairological eternity: 'When you dance with me, we dance forever' (*Hit Music*). But the Pet Shop Boys are also well aware that, ultimately, this is escapism: 'Live a lie, dance forever.' It gives some consolation, but no solution. The aesthetic revelation – like the anaesthetic revelation – is at most temporary. The Pet Shop Boys' album *Bilingual* takes us from an opening question in *Discoteca*: 'Is there a disco around?' to the final song *Saturday Night Forever*, where one has entered the club. But as the penultimate track says: 'I know that it's not gonna last forever.' They have a Schopenhauer-like belief in music but, like Schopenhauer, know that it will not last. The music *must* carry on, but *cannot* carry on, just like Beckett's voice has to carry on despite the fact that it cannot. When one is not out clubbing, there is nothing to do but to try to live an everyday life, in boredom and waiting, yet with hope. Music, or anything else in the aesthetic dimension, is not a solution in itself.

In *Zen and the Art of Motorcycle Maintenance* Robert Pirsig simply recommended sleep as a means of combating boredom.[19] Obviously, this must work, but the effect is unfortunately only temporary, and hardly relevant for anything except situative boredom. If one is bored at a lecture, it helps to have a sleep. Also if one is reading a boring book. But one cannot just sleep all the time.

Arnold Gehlen claimed that only reality helps against boredom.[20] That is by no means a bad suggestion, but it is not possible to get hold of a piece of reality just like that. The problem with boredom, among other things, is that one 'loses' reality. Gehlen's proposal could seem to be a solution that assumes the problem has already been solved. But to *experience* boredom is to experience a piece of reality. Rather than immediately happen on an antidote to boredom, there could be some point in lingering and maybe finding some kind of meaning in boredom itself. It is not possible to completely deselect boredom or some other mood, but one can choose to recognize it or to repress it. Bertrand Russell reckoned that 'a generation that cannot endure boredom will be a generation of little men.'[21] I think he is right here. And without the ability to tolerate a certain degree of boredom one will live a miserable life, because life will be lived as a continuous flight from boredom. So all children ought to be brought up to be able to be bored. To activate a child at all times is to neglect an important part of child-rearing.[22]

Joseph Brodsky provides the recipe that would seem to be the most convincing: 'When boredom strikes, throw yourself into it. Let it squeeze you, submerge you, right to the bottom.'[23] That is good advice, but difficult to follow, for it goes against every fibre in your being not to try and shrug yourself free of boredom. Boredom contains a potential. In boredom an emptying takes place, and an emptiness can be a receptiveness, although it does not have to be it. Boredom pulls things out of their usual contexts. It can open ways up for a new configuration of things, and therefore also for a new meaning, by virtue of the fact that it has already deprived things of meaning. Boredom, because of its negativity, contains the possibility of a positive turnaround. As I've mentioned before, boredom gives you a perspective on your own existence, where you realize your own insignificance in the greater context. Here is Brodsky:

> For boredom is time's invasion of your world system. It puts your life into perspective, and the net result is precisely insight and humility. The former gives rise to the latter, nota bene. The more you learn about your own format, the humbler and more sympathetic you become to your fellow-beings, to this dust that swirls in the sun's ray or that already lies motionless on your table top.[24]

The problem for the Romantic is precisely that he does not recognize his own size; he has to be bigger than everything else, transgress all boundaries and devour the whole world. That is why Romanticism ends in barbarism. And it is boundaries that do something important. As E. M. Cioran has pointed out, 'We cannot conceive eternity except by eliminating all that is transitory, all that *counts* for us.'[25] If we were immortal, existence would be devoid of meaning.

Boredom is boring because it seems infinite, but this infinity is one that meets us in this life and is thus able to show us our own finitude. Choices are important because we cannot take an infinite number of them. The more choices and potential choices, the less will each choice signify. Surrounded by an infinite selection of 'interesting' objects that can be chosen so as to be discarded, nothing will have any value. For that reason, immortality would have been immensely boring, for it would allow an infinite number of choices.

Every life contains fragmentation, and it is hardly possible to imagine a life that is completely integrated. Life can, however, become so fragmented that it almost ceases to be a life, for a life must always have a certain amount of uniformity, a certain narrative thread. It is also clear that we are more fragmented at some times of our lives than at others. There is reason to believe that fragmentation has increased in modernity and that it is continuing to increase. Self-identity is inextricably bound up with the identity of the surroundings. A fragmentation in the one leads to a fragmentation in the other. In loneliness there is a possibility of putting the self back together. Loneliness, on the other hand, can also be destructive. Isolation is a terrible punishment, and loneliness can seem conducive to disintegration rather than integration. When loneliness increases, one clings to whatever, or whoever, is capable of banishing it. It is as if we are attempting to drown out the inner voice that says that life is not functioning. But the voice is still there when the drowning-out mechanism ceases to function.

I do not claim to have a recipe as to how one can establish a genuine self. In addition, self-reflection is a task one ought to carry out oneself without getting a set recipe from someone else. For me, philosophy is the designation of a subject rather than reflective work. A subject can be taught to others, while reflective work is always something each person has to do for himself or herself. As Wittgenstein said, 'Working with philosophy is . . . really more about working with oneself. With one's own conceptions. With how one looks at things. (And what one expects of them.)'[26] There would be something very wrong about delegating a self-reflection.

As I see it, Pascal was right in saying that boredom contains self-insight, or rather the *possibility* of self-insight. Or, as Nietzsche put it: 'He who completely entrenches himself against boredom also entrenches himself against himself.'[27] One becomes alone in boredom because one cannot find any foothold outside oneself, and in profound boredom one does not even find a foothold inside oneself. From a historical point of view, loneliness has often been viewed positively, because it was so well-suited for abandoning oneself to God, to intellectual considerations and to self-examination. Very few people, however, have a positive view of loneliness nowadays. Can this be due to the fact, as Odo Marquard claims, that we are well on the way to losing our 'capacity for loneliness'?[28] Instead of loneliness we embrace self-centredness, and in self-centredness we are dependent on the looks of others and try to fill in their entire field of vision, thereby seeking to affirm ourselves. The self-centred person never has time for him- or herself, only for the reflection of him- or herself s/he can find in others. The self-centred person never finds any peace in relation to his or her own shrinking little self, but is forced to inflate an outer self to enormous proportions – and this is a gigantic self that becomes ever more difficult to keep track of for the person who has invented it. Paradoxically, the self-centred person becomes lonelier than the one that accepts loneliness, for the former is only surrounded by mirrors, while the lonely person can find room for others that are genuine. The self-centred person can only think 'It isn't easy to be me', while the lonely person is able to realize that it is not easy to be anyone at all.

Loneliness is not, of course, a good thing in itself. It is often experienced as a burden, but it also contains a potential. All humans are lonely, some more than others, but no one escapes loneliness. The crucial thing is how it is encountered, whether it is encountered as a restless absence or as a possibility for serenity. Olaf Bull has written about 'the fine, sensitive mind of loneliness'.[29] In loneliness there is a possibility of being in equilibrium with oneself rather than seeking equilibrium in things and people that have such a high velocity that they constantly slip away.

Perhaps the feeling of loss I mentioned earlier can be seen as a feeling of conscience, a feeling of an obligation I have to live a more substantial life. Perhaps boredom tells me that I am throwing away my life. In boredom life feels like a nothingness because life is being lived as a nothingness. The Norwegian concept of *samvittighet* (conscience) comes from the German *Gewissen*, which is a translation of the Latin *conscientia*, which in turn is synonymous with the Greek *syneidesis*. All of these words have something in common, something their prefixes (*sam-*, *ge-*, *con-*, *syn-*) confirm. All these words mean a con-science, a knowledge about oneself. We are talking about observing ourselves and passing judgements on our own actions. Conscience belongs to loneliness, for in the last resort it is always *I* who am guilty. Even though loneliness is universally human, it is utterly personal. It has to do with me and, at times, it *is* me. Just as loneliness and conscience are mine, boredom is also *my* boredom. It is a boredom for which I have the responsibility.

Conscience is conducive to reflecting on the life one is leading. And that takes time. Nowadays, where efficiency is one of the great buzz words, we prefer everything to move at a brisk pace, but that is not how things are when it comes to processing that which deeply affects us. That *must* take time. If not, there is some essential that is lacking. The outer conditions are not particularly favourable for dwelling on boredom, for part of the experiencing of boredom is that it takes time. Instead of allowing ourselves that time, we choose to banish it. Does one become happy via all the diversions – the holidays, TV, drink, drugs, promiscuity? Hardly, but most of us are at least a bit less unhappy for a while. Even so, one asks oneself: What value do these pleasures have, except as a way of passing the time? We can imagine being able to keep the pleasure centre of the brain constantly stimulated, so that life would be a unbroken fun trip from life to death, but that would appear to be far too unworthy. To renounce the pain of living is to dehumanize oneself. We feel a need to justify our existence, and a series of discrete shallow experiences is simply not enough. Even if we can justify all our individual actions, the problem of justifying the whole of these actions remains – i.e., the life we lead. It is our duty to lead a life that *torments* us. At the same time, this life is always somewhere else, to borrow an expression from Kundera. The obligation to live a life leads us inevitably back to boredom. A kind of moral of boredom arises. To remain in boredom because it contains an echo of a promise of a better life.

In his earlier notebooks Wittgenstein wrote that 'Man can make himself happy just like that.'[30] For him, this is linked to a Schopenhauerian point, that we must give up having any influence over actions in the world. I do not believe this is correct. I do not believe that of ourselves, via a positive or negative effort of will, we can simply make ourselves happy or that others can complete the task for us. Thirty years on, Wittgenstein said this:

> The solution of the problem you see in life is a way of living which makes what is problematic disappear.
>
> The fact that life is problematic means that your life does not fit life's shape. So you must change your life, & once it fits the shape, what is problematic will disappear.

But don't we have the feeling that someone who does-n't see a problem there is blind to something important, indeed to what is most important of all?

Wouldn't I like to say he is living aimlessly – just blindly like a mole as it were; & if he could only see he would see the problem?

Or shouldn't I say: someone who lives rightly does not experience the problem as sorrow, hence not after all as a problem, but rather as joy, that is so to speak as a bright halo around his life, not a murky background.[31]

How can one get oneself to live in such a way that the problems of life disappear? There is no universal recipe available. And how can it be at all possible to live a life that it not problematic? The crucial thing is to find a perspective where one can live *with* the problems without becoming a 'miserabilist', one who lives *for* them. It is going far too far if, like philosophers from Schopenhauer to Zapffe, one claims that existence of necessity is meaningless or tragic, or that every happiness is merely an illusion – as, for example, Leopardi unceasingly insisted. A number of people actually find meaning in existence, and it is not the task of philosophers and others to point out that their lives 'actually' are meaningless. Ecclesiastes states that 'For in much wisdom is much grief: and he that increaseth knowledge increaseth sorrow.'[32] Even though Solomon was a wise man, I believe that he – along with the author of the *Håvamål* and many more[33] – are wrong in claiming that there is an obvious connection between wisdom and melancholy. For the melancholy person there may possibly lie consolation in imagining an extraordinary profundity in one's own mental life, though this is probably most often a false consolation. One can be happy without being a shallow person. Although it is more common, however, to be unhappy *and* shallow. At the same time, I would like to emphasise that it is not a philosophical task to point out to people that their melancholy is illusory. I have never been able to stand people who insist on lighting a candle whenever I curse the dark. They are simply showing a lack of respect for the darkness that surrounds many people's lives. The dark, too, is a genuine experience, although I think T. S. Eliot is right when he lets the unknown guest in *The Cocktail Party* state that there is ultimately no other reason for staying in the dark than for getting rid of the idea that one has ever been in the light.[34]

It is possible that happiness is close at hand, but as Hölderlin said in *Der Ister* (The Danube):

Not without wings
Can anyone catch hold of what is closest
Just like that
And gain the other side.[35]

After all, it lies beyond human will-power to find a way out of boredom. It is also symptomatic that it is the outbreak of war that wrenches Hans Castorp out of his seven-year doze in *The Magic Mountain*. Boredom cannot be overcome by some simple sleight of hand, but neither are we hopelessly condemned to suffer it. It is possible to live with it. Every attempt to directly escape from boredom will, to all appearances, only make it worse in the longer term, and every DIY recipe for anti-boredom medicine ought to be met with the greatest scepticism.[36] All the cures that are recommended against boredom – such as art, love or a relationship to God – are probably things that should be sought for their own sake and do not deserve to be reduced to a mere flight from boredom.

I have not written all that much about boredom and children so far, despite the fact that it is an important subject. There are others better qualified than I am to undertake such a task.[37] It has probably also something to do with my own attempt to become adult. Like most readers of this book, I will never grow up. In spite of the fact I decided not to offer you any introduction to the Art of Living – for I would scarcely be able to provide a good example – the attempt to become adult is perhaps worth considering.

Childhood has not always existed. It is, as Philippe Ariès has shown, not more than roughly 300 years old.[38] It was discovered back then that a child is not a 'miniature adult' but something else – a child. It is possible that this was a fateful discovery. As far as our subject-matter is concerned, it is very curious that childhood and boredom emerge at approximately the same time. I would not claim that there is an unambiguous connection between the emergence of these two phenomena, but it is a coincidence that is worth making a mental note of. With Romanticism – building on the thoughts of Rousseau – childhood becomes an ideal. The true human being, not yet ruined by civilization, is now the child. Becoming adult, from a Romantic point of view, is almost to be seen as a dehumanization process. To become old is, so to speak, an attack on our personal integrity – and eternal youth is at the top of our want list. 'Youth' is an even more recent construction than 'the child', and is perhaps a greater ideal for our age than 'the child' is. We can also observe that fashion changed towards the end of the eighteenth century, suddenly having as its prime objective the power to make people look visually younger rather than older. Practically all advertising nowadays is youth-oriented. If advertising should speak to the older generation, it is because it wants to offer them a product that can make them look or feel younger.

I suspect that much of our metaphysical grief, the loss of experience I described earlier, is the grief of a lost childhood. That, at least, is what immediately suggests itself. As Kierkegaard wondered: 'My unhappiness at the present is that I am jealous of the past.'[39] But it is just as immediate to consider this lack of childhood as a lack of world, i.e., that the experience of loss in relation to childhood is symptomatic of a loss of world. Confusing the two, we insist – as does the child – on being entertained, that attention is constantly filled with something 'interesting'. We refuse to accept that we gradually have to leave the magic world of childhood, where so much is new and exciting. Once more, we are suspended somewhere between childhood and maturity, in an eternal adolescence – and adolescence is stuffed with boredom. Since childhood has been lost for good, it is more promising to crane forward towards maturity.

It was Kant who explicitly established the connection between maturity and Enlightenment by defining authority as a transgression of self-inflicted immaturity.[40] And it is tempting to say that the slogan of the Enlightenment has been taken from Shakespeare: 'Ripeness is all.'[41] From a Hegelian point of view, maturity should be understood as a self-realization in an already-existing society, but the fragmentation of modernity has undermined the belief that such a uniform ethical society is possible. This means that maturity would also seem to be unrealizable. The question is whether we can find some other conception of maturity. Nietzsche talks about his doctrine of eternal recurrence as the 'new Enlightenment',[42] thereby making clear that he wants to establish a new conception of maturity. He claims that one's maturity depends on having 'reacquired the seriousness that one had as a child at play'.[43] In this light, Nietzsche would seem to be continuing the Romantic project. His conscience says one single thing to him: 'We [...] should seek to become what we are.'[44] And who you really *are*, according to Nietzsche, is a child – a large child that can turn life into an aesthetical game and affirm itself in all perpetuity. Maturity consists in establishing a self, and as far as Nietzsche was concerned, this is a matter of 'giving style' to one's character.[45] He claimed that 'As an aesthetic phenomenon existence is *endurable* to us.'[46] But Nietzsche's conception of maturity, with its *amor fati*,[47] is extreme – too extreme for us who are all too human. It is one thing to accept one's fate, another thing to love it.

Foucault's conception of maturity is far more human, but is based on the same aestheticism as Nietzsche's. The project of Enlightenment, as defined by Kant, consisted – as mentioned – of bringing humanity to the point of maturity – becoming of age. Foucault agreed with the project, but he also underlined that Enlightenment did not lead to any maturity. He also doubted if we will ever manage to become adult.[48] So far I agree with Foucault, but I believe that the transgressive aestheticism he proposed is part of the problem, not the solution to it. Where Kant's critical project focused on the question of what boundaries knowledge *cannot* go beyond, Foucault's criticism is a practical investigation of various potential transgressions.[49] The ideal – and the only ethical task – becomes an aesthetical one: 'To create oneself as a work of art'.[50]

Foucault's self is a self constantly striving to overcome itself. This is reminiscent of Kafka's little fable, where a man asks his servant to saddle his horse, and when the servant asks him where he is off to, he replies: 'Away from here, that is my goal!'[51] Foucault's self can never find rest. There is no absolute process of emancipation, for the subject always wishes to be bound to its historical situation, but it is a *never-ending* process of emancipation. It is as if Foucault imitated Hölderlin's words, that the glory of man is never to be satisfied. The non-Romantic aspect of Foucault is that he recognized the limits of reality, that they cannot be placed and replaced as the subject sees fit, and that dissimilar historical situations allow for different transgressions. Foucault's self does not bet all its money on a Messianic hope, but involves itself in the concrete historical situation.

Even though Foucault explicitly placed himself within the framework of Kant's critical project and has been a far better interpreter of Kant's thought than most people realize, it has to be admitted that his transformation of Kant's critical *ethos* is a Romanticization and, as such, also an infantilization. Foucault's subject will never fully mature, because all maturity will seem to be boring, without the intensities and transgressions the Romantic self demands. Maturity calls for constancy, that one, *after due reflection*, to a great extent remains the person one was, which for the Romantic will always seem to be pitifully boring. To remain the same is, however, to create something that is at least a fragment of a history. We can hardly do anything else than maintain the present. This is a less overwrought version of Nietzsche's *amor fati* – an acceptance of what is given, a confirmation of actual boundaries, with the aim of *not* transgressing them. To become mature is to accept that life cannot remain in the enchanted realm of childhood, that life to a certain extent is boring, but at the same time to realize that this does not make life unliveable. This does not, of course, solve anything, but it changes the nature of the problem.

Postscript

In the Preface I claimed that this book would comprise more a series of sketches than a cohesive argument that led to a conclusion. What should such a conclusion be like? That human life is boring? Well, life often *is* boring. Different people are afflicted by boredom to differing degrees, but it is practically impossible not to be affected by boredom sooner or later. If boredom strikes hard, one is inevitably brought to an existential borderline situation where one has to question the nature of one's entire existence.

The focus of a book on boredom as a phenomenon of modernity could possibly induce the reader to believe that I wanted to tell a story of decline. But this is not so. I do not think it is possible to compare various historical eras and call them better or worse than others. My aim has been to emphasise boredom as a major problem in modernity. Boredom becomes widespread when traditional structures of meaning disappear. In modernity the subject is released from tradition and has to seek new meanings for itself. The modern subject does so via transgressions of various kinds, but is left more bereft after each new transgression. This was illustrated in the analyses of *William Lovell*, *American Psycho* and *Crash*. Boredom and lack of meaning finally almost coincide, with the modern subject believing that this meaning can be acquired by transgressing the self, by making all other accessible meaning one's own.

Personal meaning, understood as a unique meaning for me, as something that alone can give my life meaning, turns out to be unrealizable. We can quite well wait a life-time for this meaning, but it never comes. That is Beckett's problem. Warhol showed us that the need for such a meaning is ineradicable. We seem to be left in a situation where we are helplessly thrown back on boredom – as if we only have the possibility of choosing between boredom and a number of 'interesting' replacements that, in the long run, bring us back to the same boredom. Let us not forget, how-ever, that boredom, despite everything, is only one aspect of existence. Everything else does not deserve to be reduced to simply representing the boring or the interesting.

Nor does boredom refer to a great hidden meaning, as Heidegger imagined. It springs from a lack of meaning, but such a lack cannot guarantee that there is something that can fill it. In Heidegger's perspective, boredom itself acquires meaning because, as long as it becomes truly profound, it effects a turn-around to another mode of being, another time – the Moment. As Beckett shows, the Moment is always indefinitely postponed. The Moment – the actual Meaning of life – only appears in a negative form, that of absence, and the small moments (in love, art, intoxication) never last long. The problem, first and foremost, lies in accepting that all that is given are small moments and that life offers a great deal of boredom between these moments. For life does not consist of moments but of time. The absence of the great Meaning does not, however, result in all meaning in life evaporating. A one-sided focusing on the absence of Mean-ing can overshadow all other meaning – and then the world really looks as if it has been reduced to rubble. A source of profound boredom is that we demand capital letters where we are obliged to make do with small ones. Even though no Meaning is given, there is meaning – and boredom. Boredom has to be accepted as an unavoidable fact, as life's own gravity. This is no grand solution, for the problem of boredom has none.

References

PREFACE

1   Arthur Rimbaud, *A Season in Hell*, trans. Paul Schmitt (Boston, New York, Toronto and London, 1997), p. 21.
2   *Ibid.*, p. 31.
3   Emmanuel Levinas, *Of God Who Comes to Mind*, trans. Bettina Bergo (Stanford, CA, 1998), p. 7.

ONE: The Problem of Boredom

1   Jon Hellesnes, *På grensa: Om modernitet og ekstreme tilstandar* (Oslo, 1994), p. 15.
2   Aristotle, *Ethica Nicomachea*, 1112a31.
3   Oscar Levy, ed., *The Complete Works of Friedrich Nietzsche*, vol. VII: *Human, All Too Human*, 2 vols, trans. Helen Zimmern and Paul V. Cohn (London, 1909), §2, p. 15.
4   Aristotle, *Ethica Nicomachea*, 1103a24.
5   For anyone wishing to read a more personal contribution to boredom, I would recommend Peter Handke's brilliant little book *Über die Müdigkeit* (Frankfurt am Main, 1989).
6   Fernando Pessoa, *The Book of Disquiet*, trans. and ed. Richard Zenith (London, 2001), section 78, p. 76.
7   Georges Bernanos, *Tagebuch eines Landpfarrers* (Berlin, 1970), p. 8; the English translation, *The Diary of a Country Priest*, was published in 1937, one year after the original appeared.
8   Sigmund Freud, 'Mourning and Melancholia', in *On Metapsychology*, vol. XI of the Pelican Freud Library, trans. J. Strachey and ed. Angela Richards (Harmondsworth, 1984), p. 254.
9   See, for example, Orrin Klapp, *Overload and Boredom* (New York, 1986), p. 24.

10 Adam Phillips, *On Kissing, Tickling and Being Bored: Psychoanalytic Essays on the Unexamined Life* (London, 1993), p. 82.

11 Lord Byron, *Don Juan* (Harmondsworth, 1973), Canto XIV, 18.

12 See, for example, William L. Mikulas and Stephen J. Vodanovich, 'The Essence of Boredom', *Psychological Record*, I (1993).

13 Arthur Schopenhauer, 'Parerga und Paralipomena I', in *Sämtliche Werke* (Frankfurt am Main, 1986), vol. IV, pp. 581, 587.

14 Levy, *Nietzsche*, VII: *Human, All Too Human*, §391, p. 297.

15 Søren Kierkegaard, *Either-Or Part I*, trans. Howard V. Hong and Edna H. Hong (Princeton, NJ, 1987).

16 Hellesnes, *På grensa*, pp. 21–2.

17 Ezra Pound, *The Cantos: Revised Collected Edition* (London, 1975), Canto LIII.

18 Robert Nisbet, 'Boredom', in *Prejudices: A Philosophical Dictionary* (Cambridge, MA, and London, 1982), p. 26.

19 See, for example, Winsome Rose Gordon and Luise Caltabiano, 'Urban–Rural Differences in Adolescent Self-Esteem, Leisure Boredom, and Sensation Seeking as Predictors of Leisure-Time Usage and Satisfaction', *Adolescence*, XXXI (1997); Deborah E. Rupp and Stephen J. Vodanovich, 'The Role of Boredom Proneness in Self-Reported Anger and Aggression', *Journal of Social Behaviour and Personality*, IV (1997); Mikulas and Vodanovich, 'The Essence of Boredom'.

20 Ludvig Holberg, 'Om det melankolske temperament', in *Essays* (Oslo, 1994), p. 71.

21 See Oswald Bayer, *Zeitgenosse im Widerspruch: Johann Georg Hamann als radikaler Aulklärer* (Munich and Zurich, 1988), pp. 217–28.

22 E. M. Cioran, *Gevierteilt* (Frankfurt am Main, 1982), p. 77; cf. Nietzsche, 'Menschliches, Allzumenschliches', in *Kritische Studienausgabe* (Munich, Berlin and New York, 1988), vol. II, § 283f.

23 Ludwig Wittgenstein, *Philosophical Investigations*, trans. G.E.M. Anscombe (Oxford, 1953), § 123, p. 49.

24 Martin Heidegger, *Grundfragen, der Philosophie: Ausgewählte 'Probleme' der 'Logik'* (Frankfurt am Main, 1992), p. 153.

25 Samuel Beckett, *Dream of Fair to Middling Women*, ed. Eoin O'Brien and Edith Fournier (Dublin, 1992), p. 121.

26 Pessoa, *The Book of Disquiet*, section 263, p. 229.

27 Peter Wessel Zapffe, *Om det tragiske* (Oslo, 1996).

28 Kierkegaard, *Either/Or*, p. 286.

29 Nietzsche, 'Menschliches, Allzumenschliches', *Der Wanderer und sein Schatten*, § 56.

30 Friedrich Nietzsche, 'Der Antichrist', in *Kritische Studienausgabe*

(Munich, Berlin and New York, 1988), vol. VI, § 48.

31 Henry David Thoreau, 'Walden, or Life in the Woods' and 'Civil Disobedience', intro. Michael Meyer (Harmondsworth, 1983), p. 52.

32 Alberto Moravia, La Noia (Reinbek, 1990), p. 9.

33 Immanuel Kant, 'Pädagogik', in Kants gesammelte Schriften (Berlin and New York, 1902–), vol. IX, p. 471.

34 Nisbet, 'Boredom', p. 25.

35 Ecclesiastes, I:2 and I:9. For these and other biblical quotations the King James version has been used.

36 Arne Garborg, Trette menn [Weary Men] (Oslo, 1991), pp. 208–9.

37 See, for example, Seneca's 'On Tranquility of Mind', in The Stoic Philosophy of Seneca, ed. Moses Hadas (New York, 1968), pp. 75–106.

38 For a fine development of this motif, with the main emphasis on melancholy, see Wolf Lepenies, Melancholie und Gesellschaft (Frankfurt am Main, 1969, new edn 1998).

39 François de La Rochefoucauld, Maxims, trans. Leonard Tancock (Harmondsworth, 1959), § 555.

40 For a typical formulation of this, see Ludwig Wittgenstein, 'Vermischte Bemerkungen', in Werkausgabe, vol. VIII (Frankfurt am Main, 1994), p. 459.

41 For an overview of some of the statistical material available, see Klapp, Overload and Boredom, p. 24.

42 Hans-Georg Gadamer, 'Über leere und erfüllte Zeit', in Neuere Philosophie – Probleme – Gestalten, Gesammelte Werke (Tübingen 1987), vol. IV, pp. 141–2.

43 See Klapp, Overload and Boredom, p. 25.

44 This information is to be found in Ordbog over det danske sprog [Dictionary of the Danish Language] (Copenhagen, 1928). I would like to thank Åsta Norheim from the Norwegian Language Council for passing this information to me.

45 Norsk Riksmålsordbok [Dictionary of the Standard Norwegian Language] (Oslo, 1983), vol. XI, p. 2397.

46 From Kierkegaard's Either-Or.

47 Feodor Dostoevsky, Notes from the Underground; or see Aus dem Dunkel der Grossstadt (Frankfurt am Main, 1986), p. 25.

48 Georg Büchner, 'Leonce und Lena', in Sämtliche Werke, Briefe und Dokumente in zwei Bänden (Frankfurt am Main, 1992), I, p. 96.

49 Georg Büchner, 'Lenz', in Sämtliche Werke, p. 244.

50 Stendhal, Über die Liebe [On Love] (Frankfurt am Main, 1975), p. 288.

51 Pessoa, from The Book of Disquiet.

52 Bertrand Russell, The Conquest of Happiness (London, 1932), p. 57.

53 See Klapp, Overload and Boredom, chap. 10.

54 For a thorough account of various replacements for meaning, see
    Zapffe, *Om det tragiske*, chap. 6.
55 Cf. Joseph Brodsky, 'In Praise of Boredom', in *On Grief and Reason*
    (New York, 1995).
56 For a sophisticated discussion of the relationship between knowledge
    and interest, where admittedly the main emphasis is on more general
    than personal interests, see Jürgen Habermas, *Technik und
    Wissenschaft als Ideologie* (Frankfurt am Main, 1995), p. 14ff.
57 Martin Heidegger, *Was heisst Denken?* (Tübingen, 1984), p. 2;
    Vorträge und Aufsätze (Pfullingen, 1990), p. 125.
58 See Seán Desmond Healy, *Boredom, Self and Culture* (London and
    Toronto, 1984), p. 24.
59 Karl Philipp Moritz, 'Fragmente aus dem Tagebuch eines
    Geistersehers', in *Werke* (Frankfurt am Main, 1981), vol. III, p. 291. The
    theme of boredom also appears frequently in Moritz's literary works
    (especially in the novels *Anton Reiser* and *Andreas Hartknopf*), but,
    surprisingly, it is dealt with only to a lesser extent in his psychologi-
    cal studies.
60 Walter Benjamin, 'The Storyteller', in *Illuminations*, ed. Hannah
    Arendt, trans. Harry Zohn (London, 1992), p. 86.
61 *Ibid.*, pp. 88–9.
62 Benjamin, 'On Some Motifs by Baudelaire', in *Illuminations*, pp. 155–6.
63 T. S. Eliot, 'Choruses from "The Rock" (1934)', in *The Complete Works
    and Plays* (London, 1987), p. 147.
64 It is also relevant here to include the linguistic philosophy of Ernst
    Jünger in 'Der Arbeiter' (1932), in *Sämtliche Werke*, vol. VI (Stuttgart,
    1960). He claims that technology is the language of the present age –
    'a primitive language that is convincing by its mere existence' (p.
    177). In other words, it is a language that makes every hermeneutic
    dimension superfluous, for it has no meaning that has to be extract-
    ed via any interpretation.
65 Zapffe, *Om det tragiske*, p. 65.
66 Zapffe, 'We make the metaphysical demand of life . . . that it be full
    to the brim with a meaning for everything that occurs, with every-
    thing there is of experiencing consciousness in us, which we experi-
    ence as being inalienable and which constitute the specific nature of
    our being, our unique world-historical opportunity, our pride and
    nobility.' (*ibid.*, p. 100).
67 It must be underlined here that pre-modern societies are also char-
    acterized by a number of various forms of disfunctionality and that
    one ought to avoid considering them as something uniform and
    completely harmonious, but boredom and emptiness of meaning do

not seem to be a great problem in such societies.

68 Max Horkheimer and Theodor W. Adorno, *Dialektik der Aufklärung* (Frankfurt am Main, 1981), p. 112.

69 For an account that contradicts this, see Françoise Wemelsfelder, *Animal Boredom: Towards an Empirical Approach of Animal Subjectivity* (Leiden, 1993).

70 Nisbet, 'Boredom', p. 23.

71 It should be noted here that both the word and the phenomenon have a long prehistory. For an informative and relatively simple presentation, see Michael Allan Gillespie, *Nihilism before Nietzsche* (Chicago, 1995). Jacobi's letter is available in a number of editions, for example, in Friedrich Heinrich Jacobi, 'Brief an Fichte', in *Werke*, vol. III (Darmstadt, 1968).

72 Feodor Dostoevsky, *The Possessed*, vol. XI; or see *Die Dämonen* (Frankfurt am Main, 1986), p. 852.

73 Fernando Pessoa, *The Book of Disquiet*, trans. and ed. Richard Zenith (London, 2001), section 445, p. 365.

74 Theodor W. Adorno, *Minima Moralia: Reflexionen aus dem beschädigten Leben* (Frankfurt am Main, 1970), pp. 230–31.

75 Milan Kundera, *Identity*, trans. Linda Asher (London, 1988), p. 75.

76 Charles Baudelaire, *Les Fleurs du mal*, ed. J. Gilly (Paris, 1963), p. 145.

77 Walter Benjamin, 'Zentralpark', in *Gesammelte Schriften* (Frankfurt am Main, 1991), vol. I, p. 668.

78 Pat Doyle *et al.*, *The Paint House: Words from an East End Gang* (Harmondsworth, 1977), p. 31.

79 Benjamin, 'The Work of Art in the Age of Mechanical Reproduction', in *Illuminations*, p. 235.

80 Nisbet, 'Boredom', p. 28.

81 Georges Bernanos, *Tagebuch*.

82 Friedrich Nietzsche, 'Nachgelassene Fragmente, 1884–1885', in *Kritische Studienausgabe* (Munich, Berlin and New York, 1988), vol. XI, pp. 267–8.

83 Brodsky, 'In Praise of Boredom', in *On Grief and Reason*.

84 Simone Weil, 'The Power of Words', in *The Simone Weil Reader*, ed. George A. Panichas (1985).

85 Kundera, in *Identity*.

86 Martin Doehlemann, *Langeweile? Deutung eines verbreiteten Phänomens* (Frankfurt am Main, 1991), pp. 22–3.

87 Gustave Flaubert, *Bouvard and Pécuchet*, trans. A. J. Krailsheimer (Harmondsworth, 1976).

88 Cf. Healy, *Boredom, Self and Culture*, p. 28.

89 Moravia, *La Noia*, p. 14.

90   Georges Bataille, *Die Erotik* (Munich, 1994), p. 69.

91   An obvious name to include in connection with transgression and boredom is the Marquis de Sade, whose literary production deliberately belongs to the most boring ever written, with every conceivable perversion being enumerated in a monomaniac fashion in one huge 'encyclopaedia of excess'. But precisely because it is so deliberate, his work will not be mentioned here again.

92   Arthur Schopenhauer, 'Die Welt als Wille und Vorstellung I', in *Sämtliche Werke* (Frankfurt am Main, 1986), vol. I, p. 241.

93   Franz Kafka, *Tagebücher, 1909–1923* (Frankfurt am Main, 1997), for 16 February 1915.

94   Moravia, *Lao Noia*, p. 7.

95   *Ibid.*, p. 58.

96   Martin Heidegger, 'Was ist Metaphysik?', in *Wegmarken, Gesamtausgabe* (Frankfurt am Main, 1976), vol. IX, p. 110.

97   Garborg, *Trette menn*, p. 167. Pessoa also later refers to boredom as 'a cold of the soul' in *The Book of Disquiet*.

98   Freud, 'Mourning and Melancholia', in *On Metapsychology*, vol. XI of the Pelican Freud Library.

99   Adam Phillips, *On Kissing, Tickling and Being Bored*, p. 75.

100   Pessoa, *The Book of Disquiet*, section 182, p. 161.

101   Feodor Dostoevsky, *An Author's Diary*; see *Tagebuch eines Schriftstellers*, vol. II.

102   Martin Doehlemann, *Langeweile? Deutung eines verbreiteten Phänomens* (Frankfurt am Main, 1991), p. 51.

103   This point is dealt with in detail in Klapp, *Overload and Boredom*, with the main emphasis on the information society.

104   Pessoa, *The Book of Disquiet*, p. 344.

105   Benjamin, *Zentralpark*, p. 677.

106   The best account is perhaps that of Georg Simmel, 'Philosophie der Mode' (1905), in *Gesamtausgabe* (Frankfurt am Main, 1995), vol. X, pp. 9–37. But this work is a century old, so an update would undeniably be in order.

107   *Ibid.*, p. 19.

108   For a thoughtful account of the concept of quality, see Christian Norberg-Schulz, 'Om kvalitet' [On Quality], in *Øye og hånd* (Oslo, 1997), pp. 24ff.

109   Kant, 'Anthropologie in pragmatischer Hinsicht', in *Kants gesammelte Schriften* (Berlin and New York, 1902–), vol. VII, p. 245.

110   Joris-Karl Huysmans, *A Rebours*, trans. as *Against the Grain*, ed. Havelock Ellis (New York, 1969).

111   Roland Barthes, *Das perfekte Verbrechen* (Munich, 1996), p. 12.

112 Cf. Martin Heidegger, *Einführung in die Metaphysik* (Tübingen, 1958), p. 1.
113 Jean Baudrillard, *The Perfect Crime*, trans. Chris Turner (London, 1996), p. 2.
114 Pessoa, in *The Book of Disquiet*.

TWO: Stories of Boredom

1 Such a work has yet to be written. The closest approximation so far is Reinhard Kuhn, *The Demon of Noontide: Ennui in Western Literature* (Princeton, NJ, 1976). This book is impressive when it comes to erudition, but it focuses mainly on literary texts and is not particularly systematic (most forms of melancholy are discussed at random, without any major attempt being made to distinguish between them), and recent times are touched on only briefly.
2 Much of the following information about *acedia* has been taken from Siegfried Wenzel, *The Sin of Sloth: Acedia in Medieval Thought and Literature* (Chapel Hill, NC, 1967), and Günter Bader, *Melancholie und Metapher* (Tübingen, 1990). The only Norwegian literature I am aware of is by Werner Post, 'Acedia', *Profil*, I (1992).
3 Dante Alighieri, *The Divine Comedy*, trans. H. F. Cary (London, 1814), canto VII.
4 Blaise Pascal, *Thoughts*, trans. A. J. Krailsheimer (Harmondsworth, 1966), §427, p. 129.
5 *Ibid.*, §414, p. 120.
6 *Ibid.*, §133, p. 37.
7 *Ibid.*, §622 p. 208.
8 Immanuel Kant, 'Anthropologie in pragmatischer Hinsicht', in *Kants gesammelte Schriften* (Berlin and New York, 1902–), vol. VII, p. 233.
9 *Ibid.*, p. 151.
10 *Ibid.*, p. 233.
11 Immanuel Kant, *Lectures on Ethics*, trans. Peter Heath (Cambridge, 1997), p. 154.
12 Kant, 'Anthropologie', p. 237.
13 Immanuel Kant, 'Pädagogik', in *Kants gesammelte Schriften* (Berlin and New York, 1902–), vol. IX, p. 471.
14 Kant, *Lectures on Ethics*, p. 153.
15 *Ibid.*, p. 173; cf. Kant, 'Anthropologie', p. 234.
16 Theodor W. Adorno, *Negative Dialektic*, trans. E. B. Ashton (New York, 1973), p. 370.
17 Tor Ulven, *Avløsning* [Relief] (Oslo, 1993), p. 137.

18 Kant, *Lectures on Ethics*, p. 153.

19 Thomas Mann, *The Magic Mountain*, trans. H. T. Lowe-Porter (Harmondsworth, 1977), p. 104.

20 Kierkegaard, *Either-Or Part I*, trans. Howard V. Hong and Edna H. Hong (Princeton, NJ, 1987), p. 290

21 *Ibid.*, p. 288.

22 Arthur Schopenhauer, 'Die Welt als Wille und Vorstellung I', in *Sämtliche Werke* (Frankfurt am Main, 1986), vol. I, p. 432. For other places where Schopenhauer discusses this pendulum movement, see 'Parerga und Paralipomena I', in *Sämtliche Werke* (Frankfurt am Main, 1986), vol. IV, pp. 418–19, as well as 'Parerga und Paralipomena II', in *Sämtliche Werke* (Frankfurt am Main, 1986), vol. V, p. 438.

23 Arthur Schopenhauer, 'Die Welt als Wille und Vorstellung II', in *Sämtliche Werke* (Frankfurt am Main, 1986), vol. II, p. 629.

24 *Ibid.*, p. 430.

25 *Ibid.*, p. 429.

26 For Schopenhauer's relationship to music, see *Schopenhauer om Musikken*, ed. and trans. Peder Christian Kjerschow (Oslo, 1988).

27 Giacomo Leopardi, *Gedichte und Prosa: Ausgewählte Werke*, trans. Ludwig Wolde (Frankfurt am Main, 1981), pp. 253–4.

28 *Ibid.*, p. 177.

29 *Ibid.*, pp. 178–9.

30 *Ibid.*, pp. 177–8.

31 Friedrich Nietzsche, 'Menschliches, Allzumenschliches I', in *Kritische Studienausgabe* (Munich, Berlin and New York, 1988), vol. II, § 369; 'Der Wanderer und sein Schatten', § 56.

32 Friedrich Nietzsche, *The Joyful Wisdom*, trans. Thomas Common (Edinburgh and London, 1910), § 42, pp. 79–80.

33 Nietzsche, 'Menschliches, Allzumenschliches', § 220.

34 Oscar Levy, ed., *The Complete Works of Friedrich Nietzsche*, vol. VII: *Human, All-Too-Human*, trans. Helen Zimmern and Paul V. Cohn, 2 vols (London, 1909), pp. 385–6.

35 Cf. Friedrich Nietzsche, *Thus Spoke Zarathustra*, trans. A. Tille (London and New York, 1933), p. 285.

36 A major study is Christopher Schwarz, *Langeweile und Identität: Eine Studie zur Entstehung und Krise des romantischen Selbstgefühls* (Heidelberg, 1993). To a great extent, Schwarz draws the same lines as I do between boredom and Romanticism. He focuses on literary examples from Tieck, Schlegel and Brentano, but places less weight on the motif of transgression than I do.

37 Novalis, *Werke, Tagebücher und Briefe Friedrich von Hardenbergs* (Darmstadt, 1999), vol. I, p. 587 (letter to his brother, 27 February 1796).

38 Novalis, 'Das allgemeine Brouillon', in *Werke,* vol. II, p. 475.

39 Friedrich Schlegel, 'Critical Fragments', in *Lucinde and the Fragments,* trans. Peter Firchow (Minneapolis, MN, 1971), § 47, p. 149.

40 Friedrich Schlegel, 'Ideas', in *Lucinde and the Fragments*, trans. Firchow, § 3, p. 241.

41 See, for example, Asbjørn Aarseth, *Romantikken som konstruksjon* [Romanticism as a Construction] (Universitetsforlaget, Oslo, 1985).

42 Michel Foucault, 'The Father's "No"', in *Aesthetics, Method and Epistemology: Essential Works of Michel Foucault, 1954–1984 (*New York, 1998), vol. II, p. 18.

43 G.W.F. Hegel, *Aesthetics*, trans. T. M. Knox (Oxford, 1975), vol. I, p. 64.

44 *Ibid.*, p. 66.

45 G.W.F. Hegel, *Phenomenology of Spirit*, trans. A. V. Miller (Oxford, 1977), p. 7.

46 G.W.F. Hegel, *Enzyklopädie der philosophischen Wissenschaften I* (Frankfurt am Main, 1986), p. 79.

47 At this point, one could examine the relation between symbol and allegory in Walter Benjamin's study on the origin of German tragic drama ('Ursprung des deutschen Trauerspiels', in *Gesammelte Schriften*, vol. I, Frankfurt am Main, 1991), but it would simply take up too much space here.

48 Johann Gottlieb Fichte, *Grundzüge des gegenwärtigen Zeitalters, Gesamtausgabe der Bayerischen Akademie der Wissenschaften*, vol. VIII (Stuttgart, 1962–).

49 *Ibid.*, p. 201.

50 *Ibid.*, p. 247.

51 *Ibid.*, p. 250.

52 Immanuel Kant, 'Beantwortung der Frage, Was ist Aufklärung?', in *Kants gesammelte Schriften*, vol. VIII, p. 35.

53 Søren Kierkegaard, 'Über den Begriff der ironie', in *Gesammelte Werke*, 31 (Düsseldorf and Cologne, 1961), p. 280.

54 See Ludwig Tieck, *Der Geschichte des Herrn William Lovell* (Darmstadt, 1961). I have used the slightly abridged third edition of 1828.

55 Friedrich Schlegel, 'Athenaeum Fragments', in *Lucinde and the Fragments*, trans. Firchow, § 418, p. 230.

56 Tieck, *William Lovell*, p. 19.

57 *Ibid.*, p. 33

58 *Ibid.*, p. 187; p. 62.

59 *Ibid.*, p. 259.

60 *Ibid.*, p. 49.

61 *Ibid.*, p. 65.

62 Friedrich Hölderlin, 'Hyperions Jugend', in *Sämtliche Werke und Briefe* (Darmstadt, 1998), vol. I, p. 526.

63 *Ibid.*, p. 527.

64 See Friedrich Hölderlin, 'Hyperion – Vorletzte Fassung', in *Sämtliche Werke und Briefe*, vol. I, p. 558.

65 Martin Amis, *London Fields* (Harmondsworth, 1990), p. 26.

66 Friedrich Hölderlin, 'Hyperion', in *Sämtliche Werke und Briefe*, vol. I, p. 760.

67 Tieck, *William Lovell*, p. 83.

68 *Ibid.*, p. 160.

69 *Ibid.*, p. 88.

70 *Ibid.*, pp. 131–2.

71 *Ibid.*, p. 107.

72 *Ibid.*, p. 280.

73 *Ibid.*, pp. 238–9.

74 *Ibid.*, p. 91.

75 *Ibid.*, p. 292.

76 *Ibid.*, p. 320.

77 *Ibid.*, pp. 289–90.

78 Bret Easton Ellis, *American Psycho* (London, 1991).

79 *American Pyscho* was the subject of much criticism when it appeared. Feminists, for example, wanted to have it prohibited because of all the violence against women in the book. It ought to be noted that there is complete equality in the book: seven women and seven men are murdered by Bateman. It must be admitted, however, that the men die more swiftly than the women, and their murder is thus less brutal.

80 Stendhal, *Über die Liebe* (Frankfurt am Main, 1975), p. 283. Nietzsche later gives a description of 'the Don Juan of knowledge' that is close to this (see Friedrich Nietzsche, 'Morgenröte', in *Kritische Studienausgabe*, vol. III, Munich, Berlin and New York, 1988, § 327).

81 A later kindred spirit of Don Juan, Stavrogin, in Dostoevsky's *The Possessed*, writes in his final letter: 'I have tried all kinds of dissipations and wasted my strength on them, but I do not like and have never wished for these dissipations'.

82 Ellis, *American Psycho*, p. 377.

83 Tieck, *William Lovell*, p. 88.

84 Ellis, *American Psycho*, pp. 141, 347.

85 *Ibid.*, p. 44.

86 *Ibid.*, p. 23.

87 *Ibid.*, p. 98.

88 *Ibid.*, p. 106.

89 *Ibid.*, pp. 18, 20, 37. This is emphasized also in Ellis's most recent novel (*Glamorama*, New York, 1999, p. 38), where Patrick Bateman has a small guest appearance and is described as 'a nice guy'.

90 *Ibid.*, p. 20. Cf. pp. 216, 221, 333, 352, 388.

91 *Ibid.*, p. 71.

92 *Ibid.*, p. 238.

93 *Ibid.*, pp. 349ff.

94 *Ibid.*, p. 146.

95 *Ibid.*, p. 329.

96 *Ibid.*, pp. 374–5.

97 *Ibid.*, p. 345.

98 *Ibid.*, p. 77.

99 *Ibid.*, pp. 137, 142, 248, 264, 334, 383.

100 *Ibid.*, p. 264.

101 C. Fred Alford, *What Evil Means to Us* (Ithaca, NY, and London, 1997).

102 Ellis, *American Psycho*, p. 345.

103 *Ibid.*, p. 15.

104 *Ibid.*, p. 134.

105 *Ibid.*, p. 354.

106 *Ibid.*, p. 254.

107 *Ibid.*, pp. 150, 371, 373.

108 *Ibid.*, p. 282.

109 *Ibid.*, p. 327.

110 *Ibid.*, p. 377

111 *Ibid.*, p. 264.

112 Cf. Paul Ricoeur, *Oneself as Another*, trans. Kathleen Blamey (Chicago and London, 1992), especially pp. 141–68.

113 One could consider here Emile Durkheim's concept of *anomie* in *The Suicide*, and a number of other sociological theories that stem from this, especially in work by Robert K. Merton.

114 Simmel, 'Philosophie der Mode' (1905), in *Gesamtausgabe* (Frankfurt am Main, 1995), vol. X, p. 24.

115 Zygmunt Bauman, *Postmodern Ethics* (Oxford and Cambridge, MA, 1993), p. 244; cf. Zygmunt Bauman, *Postmodernity and its Discontents* (Cambridge, MA, 1998), chap. 6.

116 On the concept of lifestyles, see David Chaney, *Lifestyles* (London and New York, 1996).

117 Cf. Ludwig Wittgenstein, 'Vermischte Bemerkungen', in *Werkausgabe* (Frankfurt am Main, 1984), vol. VIII, p. 558.

118 Bauman, *Postmodern Ethics*, p. 241.

119 Jean Baudrillard, *The Transparency of Evil: Essays on Extreme*

     Phenomena, trans. James Benedict (London and New York, 1993), p. 16.
120 Novalis, Novalis, 'Die Christenheit oder Europa', in *Dichtungen*
     (Hamburg, 1991).
121 G.W.F. Hegel, 'Glauben und Wissen', in *Jenaer Schriften, 1801–1807*
     (Frankfurt am Main, 1986), p. 432.
122 Friedrich Nietzsche, 'Die fröhliche Wissenschaft', in *Kritische
     Studienausgabe* (Munich, Berlin and New York, 1988), vol. III, § 125.
123 See Michel Foucault, 'A Preface to Transgression', in *Aesthetics,
     Method and Epistemology: Essential Works of Michel Foucault,
     1954–1984* (New York, 1998), vol. II, p. 72.
124 J. G. Ballard, *Crash* (London, 1993), p. 8.
125 J. G. Ballard, *A User's Guide to the Millennium* (New York, 1996), p. 205.
126 *Ibid.*, p. 91.
127 *Ibid.*, p. 221.
128 Lukas Barr, 'Don't Crash: The J. G. Ballard Interview', *KGB*, 7 (1995).
129 Friedrich Mietzsche, *Zur Genealogie der Moral* (Frankfurt am Main
     and Leipzig, 1991), III § I, p. 91.
130 Arthur Miller, *The Misfits* (London, 1961), p. 51.
131 This makes one think of T. S. Eliot's 'Fragment of an Agon' in
     Sweeney Agonistes: '*Sweeney*, Birth and copulation and death. That's
     all, that's all. Birth and copulation and death. / *Doris*, I'd be bored. /
     Sweeney, You'd be bored' (*The Complete Poems and Plays*, London,
     1987, p. 122).
132 Ballard, *Crash*, p. 113.
133 Ernst Jünger, 'Der Schmerz', in *Sämtliche Werke* (Stuttgart, 1980), vol.
     VII, p. 174.
134 Karl Jaspers, Jaspers, Karl, *Psychologie der Weltanschauungen* [1919]
     (Munich and Zurich, 1994), p. 293.
135 Karl Kraus, *Nachts. Aphorismen* (Munich, 1968), p. 36.
136 Georges Bataille, *Erotism, Death and Sensuality*, trans. Mary Dalwood
     (San Francisco, 1986), p. 27.
137 Søren Kierkegaard, *Dagbøger i udvalg, 1834–1846* [Selected
     Notebooks] (Borgen, 1992), p. 291.
138 Michel Foucault, 'The Minimalist Self', in *Politics, Philosophy,
     Culture: Interviews and Other Writings, 1977–1984* (London and New
     York, 1988), p. 12.
139 Ballard, *Crash*, p. 127.
140 It is worth recalling James's description of his first meeting with
     Catherine: 'What first struck me about Catherine was her immacu-
     late cleanliness, as if she had individually reamed out every square
     centimetre of her elegant body, separately ventilated every pore. At
     time the porcelain appearance of her face, and over-elaborate make-

up like some demonstration model of a beautiful woman's face, had made me suspect that her whole identity was a charade' (*ibid.*, p. 89).

141 *Ibid.*, p. 35.
142 T. S. Eliot, 'Four Quartets' and 'Murder in the Cathedral', in *The Complete Poems and Plays* (London, 1987), pp. 172 and 271.
143 J. G. Ballard, *The Atrocity Exhibition* (London, 2001), p. 95.
144 Søren Kierkegaard, *The Repetition*, trans. Howard V. Hong and Edna H. Hong (Princeton, NJ, 1987), p. 138.
145 *Ibid.*, p. 186.
146 *Ibid.*, p. 131.
147 *Ibid.*, p. 257.
148 It is, of course, possible that the repetition of the original intimacy between James and Catherine is not a central theme at all and that we are purely and simply dealing with a death urge, although I feel that such an interpretation of the film makes it less interesting and have therefore decided to ignore it here.
149 Karl Rosenkranz, *Ästhetik des Häßlichen* (Leipzig, 1990), pp. 240–41.
150 There are, of course, exceptions, as in *Company*, where there is a long discussion of which position of the body is the least boring.
151 Samuel Beckett, *Proust* (London, 1976).
152 *Ibid.*, p. 66.
153 *Ibid.*, p. 74.
154 Samuel Beckett, 'The Unnamable', in *'Molloy', 'Malone Dies' and 'The Unnamable': Three Novels* (London, 1966), p. 309.
155 *Ibid.*, p. 316.
156 Beckett, in *Stories and Texts for Nothing*.
157 *Ibid.*.
158 Samuel Beckett, *Happy Days* (London, 1961), p. 40.
159 Samuel Beckett, *Endgame* (London, 1964), p. 13.
160 *Ibid.*, p. 29.
161 Samuel Beckett, 'Malone Dies', in *'Molloy', 'Malone Dies' and 'The Unnamable'*.
162 Beckett, *Proust*, p. 55.
163 Beckett, *Endgame*, p. 32.
164 Samuel Beckett, 'Molloy', in *Molloy, Malone Dies and The Unnamable: Three Novels* (London, 1966p. 32.
165 Beckett, in *Pour finir encore et autres foirades*.
166 Beckett, 'The Unnamable', in *'Molloy', 'Malone Dies' and 'The Unnamable'*.
167 *Ibid.*
168 Samuel Beckett, *Ohio Impromptu*, Collected Short Plays of Samuel Beckett (London, 1984), p. 285.

169 Beckett, *Endgame*, p. 32.
170 Beckett, *Stories and Texts for Nothing*.
171 *Ibid.*
172 Adorno, *Aesthetic Theory*, trans. Robert Hulot-Kentor (London, 1997), p. 30. The translation has been modified.
173 Samuel Beckett, *Watt* (London, 1963), p. 247.
174 Beckett, *Stories and Texts for Nothing*.
175 Samuel Beckett, *Worstward Ho* (London, 1983), p. 285.
176 Jean Baudrillard, *The Perfect Crime*, trans. Chris Turner (London, 1996), pp. 75–6.
177 Quoted from Victor Bockris, *The Life and Death of Andy Warhol* (London, 1998), p. 225.
178 Warhol, *The Andy Warhol Diaries*, p. 595
179 Warhol, *The Philosophy of Andy Warhol*, p. 5.
180 *Ibid.*, p. 7.
181 *Ibid.*, p. 9.
182 *Ibid.*, p. 183.
183 Quoted from Eric Shanes, *Warhol* (London, 1991), p. 18.
184 Warhol, *POPism*, p. 50.
185 Fernando Pessoa, *The Book of Disquiet*, trans. and ed. Richard Zenith (London, 2001).
186 Warhol, *The Philosophy of Andy Warhol*, p. 10.
187 *Ibid.*, p. 27.
188 *Ibid.*, p. 53.
189 *Ibid.*, p. 55.
190 *Ibid.*, p. 199.
191 *Ibid.*, p. 201.
192 See, for example, the following passage: 'It's the long life spans that are throwing all the old values and their applications out of whack. When people used to learn about sex at fifteen and die at thirty-five, they obviously were going to have fewer problems than people today who learn about sex at the age of eight or so, I guess, and live to be eighty. That's a long time to play around with the same concept. The same boring concept' (*ibid.*, p. 44).
193 Adorno, *Aesthetic Theory*, p. 32.
194 Warhol, *The Philosophy of Andy Warhol*, p. 112.
195 Warhol, *POPism*, p. 60.
196 As Emile de Antonio, who was part of Warhol circle, later said: 'He loved to see other people dying. This is what the Factory was about, Andy was the Angel of Death's Apprentice as these people went through their shabby lives with drugs and with weird sex and group sex and mass sex. So Andy looked and Andy as a voyeur *par excel-*

lence was the Devil, because he got bored just looking' (quoted from Bockris, *The Life and Death of Andy Warhol*, p. 205). Here, Warhol has a right to come with a reply: 'Now and then someone would accuse me of being evil – of letting people destroy themselves while I watched, so just I could film them and tape record them. But I don't think of myself as evil – just realistic. I learned when I was little that whenever I got aggressive and tried to tell someone what to do, nothing happened – I just couldn't carry it off. I learned that you actually have more power when you shut up, because at least that way people will start to maybe doubt themselves. When people are ready to, they change. They never do it before then, and sometimes they die before they get around to it. You can't make them change if they don't want to, just like when they want to, you can't stop them' (Warhol, *POPism*, p. 108).

197 Paul Valéry, *Mr Teste*; see *Werke* (Frankfurt and Leipzig, 1991), vol. I, p. 299.

THREE: The Phenomenology of Boredom

1 Martin Heidegger, *The Fundamental Concepts of Metaphysics, World, Finitude, Solitude*, trans. William McNeill and Nicholas Walker (Bloomington, IN, 1995).

2 This part of the book will probably make greater demands than the other sections, something that to a great extent is due to Heidegger's special terminology, which cannot immediately be translated. To facilitate access, I have chosen mainly to paraphrase Heidegger's texts as simply as possible, although it will be impossible to avoid using certain technical. The repetitive nature of his style cannot be avoided either, for it is an essential aspect of the way his thinking operates.

3 The following remarks on moods are based mainly in Martin Heidegger, *Sein und Zeit* (Tübingen, 1986), § 29.

4 Ludwig Wittgenstein, *Notebooks, 1914–16*, trans. G.E.M. Anscombe (Oxford, 1961), p. 77 (29 July 1916).

5 Wittgenstein, *Notebooks, 1914–16*, p. 78 (29 July 1916).

6 Wittgenstein seems to think that these are the two only alternatives, 'I am either happy or unhappy – that is all.' (*Ibid.*, 13 July 1916).

7 Hilary Putnam, *The Many Faces of Realism* (La Salle, PA, 1987), pp. 26ff.

8 Cf. Martin Heidegger, *Prolegomena zur Geschichte des Zeitbegriffs* (Frankfurt am Main, 1988), p. 300.

9 Cf. Ludwig Wittgenstein, 'Bemerkungen iiber die Philosophie der Psychologie I', in *Werkausgabe in 8 Bänden* (Frankfurt am Main,

1984), vol. VII, § 729.

10   E. M. Cioran, *Gevierteilt* (Frankfurt am Main, 1982), p. 130.

11   Otto Friedrich Bollnow, *Das Wesen der Stimmungen* (1941)
     (Frankfurt am Main, 1995), p. 57.

12   Cf. Otto Friedrich Bollnow, *Mensch und Raum* (Stuttgart, Berlin and
     Cologne, 1963), pp. 229–43.

13   Samuel Beckett, *Dream of Fair to Middling Women*, ed. Eoin O'Brien
     and Edith Fourmier (Dublin, 1992), p. 6.

14   It should be pointed out here that boredom can also lead to sociality,
     which serves as a diversion from boredom. Cf. Arthur Schopenhauer,
     'Parerga und Paralipomena I', in *Sämtliche Werke* (Frankfurt am
     Main, 1986), vol. IV, pp. 502ff.

15   Heidegger, *Sein und Zeit*, p. 148.

16   Cioran, *Gevierteilt*, p. 130.

17   Marcel Proust, *Remembrance of Things Past, I: Swann's Way*, trans. C.
     K. Scott Moncrieff and Terence Kilmartin (Harmondsworth, 1983),
     pp. 47–8.

18   Martin Heidegger, *Nietzsche, Erster Band* (Pfullingen, 1989), p. 119.

19   Martin Heidegger, *The Fundamental Concepts of Metaphysics, World,
     Finitude, Solitude*, trans. William McNeill and Nicholas Walker
     (Bloomington, IN, 1995), §§1–10. Heidegger is far from alone in mak-
     ing such a claim. In the *Theaititos* (155d) Plato argues that philoso-
     phy begins in *wonder*, and in the *Metaphysics* (928b) Aristotle
     emphasizes *astonishment* as the starting point. Personally, I am
     inclined to say that it is *confusion*.

20   Martin Heidegger, *Being and Time*, trans. John Macquarrie and
     Edward Robinson (Oxford, 1967), p. 246.

21   *Ibid.*

22   *Ibid.*

23   Martin Heidegger, *Phänomenologische Interpretationen zu Aristoteles,
     Einführung in die phänomenologische Forschung* (Frankfurt am Main,
     1995), p. 37.

24   Bollnow, *Das Wesen der Stimmungen*, p. 68.

25   Bollnow mentions boredom only briefly a few times in *Das Wesen
     der Stimmungen* (pp. 48, 63–4, 139, 172).

26   Martin Heidegger, *Fundamental Concepts of Metaphysics*, § 89.

27   Martin Heidegger, *Phänomenologische Interpretationen zu Aristoteles*,
     p. 72.

28   *Ibid.*, p. 109.

29   *Ibid.*, p. 15.

30   Cf. Heidegger, *Being and Time*, § 284, p. 240.

31   Heidegger, *Fundamental Concepts of Metaphysics*, §122, pp. 81–2.

32 *Ibid.*, §146, p. 97.

33 Ernst Jünger, *In Stahlgewittern* (Stuttgart, 1978), p. 237.

34 Heidegger, *Fundamental Concepts of Metaphysics*, §155, p. 102.

35 *Ibid.*, p. 105.

36 *Ibid.*, p. 108.

37 *Ibid.*, §180, p. 119.

38 *Ibid.*, p. 124.

39 *Ibid.*, p. 127.

40 *Ibid.*, p. 133.

41 *Ibid.*, p. 134.

42 Martin Heidegger, *Vier Seminare* (Frankfurt am Main, 1977), p. 137.

43 Heidegger, *Fundamental Concepts of Metaphysics*, p. 136.

44 *Ibid.*, p. 137.

45 *Ibid.*, p. 138.

46 *Ibid.*, p. 149.

47 Heidegger, *Being and Time*, §338, p. 387.

48 The First Epistle of Paul the Apostle to the Corinthians, XV: 51–2.

49 The Epistle of Paul the Apostle to the Romans, XIII: 11.

50 The First Epistle of Paul the Apostle to the Thessalonians, V: 6.

51 Cf. Heidegger, *Being and Time*, p. 310.

52 The Epistle of Paul the Apostle to the Galatians, IV: 4.

53 Martin Heidegger, *Phänomenologie des religiösen Lebens* (Frankfurt am Main, 1995), p. 82.

54 Heidegger, *Being and Time*, §310, pp. 357–8.

55 From Lorca's 'Sleepless City': 'No duerme nadie por el cielo. Nadie, nadie. / No duerme nadie. / Pero si alguien cierra los ojos, / ¡azotadlo, hijos míos, azotadlo! / Haya un panorama de ojos abiertos / y amargas llagas encendidas'.

56 Heidegger, *Fundamental Concepts of Metaphysics*, pp. 163–64.

57 *Ibid.*, p. 166.

58 *Ibid.*, p. 183.

59 Cf. Heidegger, *Einführung in die Metaphysik*, p. 1.

60 Heidegger, *Phänomenologische Interpretationen zu Aristoteles*, p. 139.

61 Heidegger, *Fundamental Concepts of Metaphysics*, p. 275.

62 *Ibid.*, p. 347.

63 Joseph Brodsky, 'In Praise of Boredom', in *On Grief and Reason* (New York, 1995), p. 109.

64 Heidegger, *Fundamental Concepts of Metaphysics*, p. 282.

65 *Ibid.*, p. 416.

66 Bollnow, *Das Wesen der Stimmungen*, p. 49.

67 Heidegger, *Fundamental Concepts of Metaphysics*, p. 172.

68 Heidegger, *Phänomenologische Interpretationen zu Aristoteles*, p. 130.

69 Heidegger, *Fundamental Concepts of Metaphysics*, p. 117.

70 Martin Heidegger, *Logik als die Frage nach dem Wesen der Sprache* (Frankfurt am Main, 1998), pp. 129–30.

71 To give an adequate account of why I believe that Heidegger's major project disintegrates falls well outside the scope of this book. For anyone interested, I would recommend Herman Philipse's work, *Heidegger's Philosophy of Being: A Critical Interpretation* (Princeton, NJ, 1998). Philipse gives a very orderly and well-informed account of all the various meanings of 'being' in Heidegger's philosophical writings, providing highly convincing arguments as to why these are mutually incompatible. See also several articles by Ernst Tugendhat on Heidegger in *Philosophische Aufsätze* (Frankfurt am Main, 1992), especially 'Heideggers Seinsfrage', pp. 108–35.

FOUR: The Ethics of Boredom

1 Milan Kundera, *Slowness*.

2 *Ibid.*.

3 Wittgenstein, 'Vermischte Bemerkungen', in *Werkausgabe* (Frankfurt am Main, 1994), vol. VIII, p. 498.

4 Cf. Richard Schacht, *The Future of Alienation* (Urbana / Chicago, IL, 1994), p. 3.

5 As Baudrillard points out in *America*, this does not only affect traditional, teleological conceptions of a Christian or Hegelian nature but even Nietzsche's doctrine of eternal recurrence: 'Even the possibility of eternal recurrence is threatened. This fantastic perspective presupposes that things are ordered in a necessary and fatal order. That is not the case today, where they are ordered in a random and transitory order'.

6 Cf. Nietzsche, 'Nachgelassene Fragmente, 1884–1885', in *Kritische Studienausgabe* (Munich, Berlin and New York, 1988), vol. XI, p. 556.

7 *Le Monde*, 7 May 1993.

8 See Hermann Broch, *Hofmannsthal und seine Zeit* (Frankfurt am Main, 2001), p. 46..

9 Oswald Spengler, *Der Mensch und die Technik* (Munich, 1971), p. 4..

10 Novalis, 'Das allgemeine Brouillon', in *Werke, Tabebücher und Briefe Friederich von Hardenbergs* (Darmstadt, 1999), vol. II, p. 676.

11 Pascal, *Thoughts*, trans. A. J. Krailsheimer (Harmondsworth, 1966), 137, p. 42.

12 Julien Gracq, *Le rivage des Syrtes* (Paris, 1951).

13 Alexis de Tocqueville, *Democracy in America*, trans. Philip Bradley

(New York, 1954), vol. II, p. 147.

14   Friedrich Schlegel, *Lucinde and the Fragments*, trans. Peter Firchow (Minneapolis, MN, 1971).

15   *Ibid.* The quotation has been slightly abridged.

16   *Ibid.*

17   *Ibid.*

18   It is naturally possible to read *Lucinde* ironically, deconstructing the love utopia and delaying the salvation indefinitely, as is the case in Tieck's *William Lovell* and in Hölderlin's *Hyperion*. This is also a reading that would accord extremely well with the rest of Schlegel's thought, but then we would also be back again in the usual, apparently endless 'dead end' of Romanticism.

19   Robert M. Pirsig, *Zen and the Art of Motorcycle Maintenance* (London, 1987), p. 310.

20   Arnold Gehlen, 'Das gestörte Zeit-Bewusstsein', *Merkur*, IV/17 (1963), p. 320.

21   Bertrand Russell, *The Conquest of Happiness* (London, 1932), p. 65.

22   Cf. Finn Skårderud, *Uro: En reise i det moderne selvet*) [Disquiet: A Journey into the Modern Self] (Oslo, 1998), pp. 408–12.

23   Brodsky, 'In Praise of Boredom', in *On Grief and Reason* (New York, 1995).

24   *Ibid.*.

25   E. M. Cioran, *Gevierteilt* (Frankfurt am Main, 1982), p. 141.

26   Wittgenstein, 'Vermischte Bemerkungen', p. 472.

27   Nietzsche, 'Menschliches, Allzumenschliches, Der Wanderer und sein Schatten', in *Kritische Studienausgabe* (Munich, Berlin and New York, 1988), vol. II, § 200.

28   Odo Marquard, 'Plädoyer für die Einsamkeitsfähigkeit', in *Von der Kraft der sieben Einsamkeiten*, ed. R. Walter (Freiburg, 1983).

29   Olaf Bull, 'Ensomhed' [Loneliness], in *Samlede dikt og noveller* (Oslo 1983), p. 56.

30   Wittgenstein, 'Tagebücher, 1914–1916', in *Werkausgabe in 8 Bänden*, vol. I (Frankfurt am Main, 1984) (14 July 1916).

31   Ludwig Wittgenstein, *Culture and Value*, ed. Georg Henrik von Wright, trans. Peter Winch (Oxford, 1998), and MS 118 17vc, 27 August 1937.

32   Ecclesiastes, I:18.

33   Here we can quote from the '*Håvamål*' in *The Edda*: 'A man ought to be of average wisdom, not too wise'. We can also mention such names as Theophrastus, Cicero, Ficino, Petrarch, Schopenhauer, Nietzsche, etc.

34   T. S. Eliot, 'The Cocktail Party', in *The Complete Poems and Plays*

(London, 1987), p. 364.

35 Friedrich Hölderlin, 'Der Ister' ('Nicht ohne Schwingen mag / Zum Nächsten einer greifen / Geradezu / Und kommen auf die andere Seite'), in *Sämtliche Werke und Briefe* (Darmstadt, 1998), vol. I, p. 475.

36 This also applies to the highly praised recipe to Mihaly Csikszentmihalyi in *Beyond Boredom and Anxiety: The Experience of Play in Work Games* (San Francisco, Washington, DC, and London, 1977), where the subject is a symbolic transformation of everyday activities, so that they are performed as play in a state of flow.

37 Cf. Adam Phillips, *On Kissing, Tickling and Being Bored: Psychoanalytic Essays on the Unexamined Life* (London, 1993); Skårderud, *Uro*, pp. 408–12.

38 Philippe Ariès, *Geschichte der Kindheit* (Munich, 1975).

39 Kierkegaard, *Dagbøger i udvalg, 1834–1846* [Selected Notebooks] (Borgen, 1992), p. 224.

40 Immanuel Kant, 'Beantwortung der Frage, Was ist Aufklärung?', in *Kants gesammelte Schriften* (Berlin and New York, 1902–), vol. VIII, p. 35.

41 William Shakespeare, *King Lear*, Act V, scene 2.

42 See, for example, Friedrich Nietzsche, 'Nachgelassene Fragmente, 1884–1885', in *Kritische Studienausgabe* (Munich, Berlin and New York, 1988), vol. XI, p. 346.

43 Friedrich Nietzsche, *Beyond Good and Evil*, trans. Helen Zimmern (London, 1909), §94, p. 89.

44 Friedrich Nietzsche, *The Joyful Wisdom*, trans. Thomas Common (London, 1910), § 270, p. 263.

45 *Ibid.*, § 290, p. 223.

46 *Ibid.*, § 107, p. 146.

47 *Ibid.*, §276, p. 213.

48 Michel Foucault, 'What is Enlightenment?', in *Ethics: Subjectivity and Truth: Essential Works of Michel Foucault, 1954–1984* (New York, 1997), vol. I, p. 262.

49 *Ibid.*, p. 315.

50 Michel Foucault, 'On the Genealogy of Ethics', in *Ethics: Subjectivity and Truth*, vol. I, p. 262

51 Franz Kafka,, 'Der Aufbruch', in *Sämtliche Erzählungen* (Frankfurt am Main 1970), p. 321.